God's peace

Robert M. Herhold

The Promise Beyond The Pain

The Promise Beyond The Pain

ROBERT M. HERHOLD

Abingdon
Nashville

THE PROMISE BEYOND THE PAIN

Library of Congress Cataloging in Publication Data

HERHOLD, ROBERT M
  The promise beyond the pain.
  1. Suffering. I. Title.
BT732.7.H4   248'.86   79-895
      ISBN 0-687-34331-3

Scripture quotations unless otherwise noted are from
the Revised Standard Version of the Bible, copyrighted
1946, 1952, © 1971, 1973 by the Division of Christian
Education of the National Council of the Churches of
Christ in the U.S.A.

Book Designer: L. B. Wooten

MANUFACTURED BY THE PARTHENON PRESS AT
NASHVILLE, TENNESSEE, UNITED STATES OF AMERICA

TO WAYNE

They that sow in tears shall reap in joy.

In our sleep, pain which cannot forget,
falls drop by drop upon the heart until,
in our own despair, against our will,
comes wisdom through the awful grace
of God.

Aeschylus

CONTENTS

PREFACE

We have all grown from suffering and have discovered that pain teaches us in ways which pleasure cannot. We find that we are uniquely open to learning when our defenses are painfully destroyed. And as we gain wisdom from such experiences, we may receive a strange joy. We learn that we can face pain, knowing we have been down that street before and that God brought some good out of it.

Joy is strange because it is not something we can manufacture for ourselves. It usually comes through other people, but it comes from beyond human sources. It is "a peace that passes understanding," a deep assurance that God loves us and works only for our good, often using pain to reach us.

It would be nice if someone could tell us precisely how to get this joy, but it defies packaging. The moment anyone tries to suggest "how to," the joy slips through our fingers like mercury. Instead we discover that joy comes without our trying, often against our will. God is always trying to give us his joy, but we often resist it. If his joy depended upon our trying to get it, what would happen when we are too discouraged or in too much pain to try? Instead of urging us to try harder, God uses any means he can to give us joy. Including pain.

This book is not an endorsement of all pain, even as a means to produce joy. Most of all, it is not about the joy of suffering. We are well rid of that strain of Christian thought. The term "pain" in this book intends to include a broad spectrum of the physical, emotional, and spiritual hurts we experience as human beings. I use the term generally without specifying kinds of pain because, for me, various pains are interrelated and pervasive. Although suffering is not to be sought, when it comes, God can use it for our welfare. Sometimes suffering appears to have no redeeming value, only pain and more pain. At other times we suffer unjustly, since we have done little or nothing to deserve it. Pain often causes us to question the goodness or the power of God. At these times, Jesus points to the cross and says, "Yes, I know, I know what you are experiencing."

Instead of a how-to book, this book is about God's strange joy which is ever "seeking us through pain." Because that joy is God-given, it is impossible to reduce it to a formula. Having received some of this joy, I feel like a prospector who knows that there is gold in "them thar hills." I cannot tell each of you how to get it out, for that requires personal exploration. Rather, this book is about the pains we all have and the joy more of us could experience.

My admiration and gratitude is unlimited for family members, parishioners, and other friends who have come through pain to wisdom and joy. I am also particularly grateful to Jean Lesher for her editorial skill and encouragement.

Rather than a map on how to find joy, we need one crazy prospector rattling some nuggets in his pan and shouting, "Gold! Gold!"

I hope this little book might start a gold rush in your life.

Robert M. Herhold
Palo Alto, California

The Promise Beyond The Pain

Chapter 1

A STRANGE JOY

Several years ago Rabbi Joshua Liebman, the author of the bestseller *Peace of Mind*, was asked by a reporter if he had peace of mind. Liebman thought for a few moments and then replied, "Yes—sometimes."

Perhaps that is all we can ask for, even, or especially, from an authority on the subject. Yet it is a fair question, and anyone professing some familiarity with a subject should be pressed for his or her personal experience. I wrote this book because it is apparent to me that a strange joy has been seeking me through whatever pain I experience. I am confident that joy comes from God and that nothing in this world can destroy it.

I have discovered that pain often serves as the vehicle of joy. I do not experience joy through all my distresses, but through enough of them so that I am confident that God uses pain to give us joy. I am slowly becoming content that "sometimes" I am joyful. Like the crazy prospector, I do not expect to strike it rich every day; but it is good to know that there is gold in the hills.

We acquire a taste for God's joy which the world cannot take away because it is not given by the world. God gives us only a taste or hint of his joy, because if he gave us any more of it, we might become too elated, as St. Paul feared about himself.

Recently I experienced a strange joy in a most unlikely situation. My irreplaceable friend, my brother Wayne, died after battling a blood disease for two years. I watched him conquer death in the last months and days of his life. The real enemy he overcame was despair. I wrote about him shortly after his death:

> I cannot write in the past tense about Wayne. He isn't *was;* he *is.* He won't even let me feel a little normal grief. Just as I do, I catch that amused twinkle in his eye and the whole thing is off. How can anyone have a good cry with a character like Wayne looking on saying: "OK, Sport, knock it off!"
>
> Wayne was so in tune with God that it was impossible for him to be irreverent. Wayne was a funny man because he sensed that God laughed with him. Once when he was feeling particularly low, I reminded him that our congregation was praying for him. He found the irony of that irresistible: "Bob, I don't want to be ungrateful, but could you tell your prayer group to knock if off for a little while? I'm not quite sure whom they are praying to." I reminded him that in his condition he couldn't afford to alienate anyone.

Wayne did not die easily or comfortably. He "raged againt the dying of the light," as Dylan Thomas said. He worked the last week of his life; there was no reason to stop living just because he was dying. He was confident that whatever happened, God was with him. His humor to the very end grew out of his strange joy. He awoke from sleep a few days before he died, opened his eyes wide and said, "Did I say anything incriminating in my sleep?" I assured him he had. "How much did I pledge to the church?" he asked.

We prayed together his last days, and once he thanked God for my sticking around. I felt I was being touched by a strange joy. When I think of Wayne, as I often do, it is impossible for me "to grieve as one who has no hope."

Despite, and even because of Wayne's death, I have tasted a joy which is addictive. No other form of joy or happiness will suffice: I have found the real thing. Wayne died wanting more life on earth, but he convinced me that death could not destroy his source of joy. I feel guilty that I should learn from Wayne's death, while, on the other hand, I have the feeling that Wayne isn't doing too badly right now; and I can hear him say: "You always knew how to make the best of a bad situation, Bob."

The hardest part of faith is to take God straight, to love him for himself, not because we want a better job, or a better marriage or better health, or to keep a brother from dying. It is difficult to trust God to give his strange joy in his time and in his fashion. Sometimes we have to endure Gethsemane and the cross a little longer before Easter comes. But living in anticipation of the resurrection, we trust that God will give us his joy in his time. The mystery of God's way is in itself a strange joy.

So much depends upon what our goal in life is. For many it is to minimize pain and to maximize pleasure. Obviously this is better than the reverse, but it is not the goal Jesus had in mind. For him eternal life or joy is to know God, and so he prayed, "And this is eternal life, that they know thee the only true God, and Jesus Christ whom thou has sent." Pain or pleasure is not the first consideration for the Christian; rather it is knowing God.

Knowing God means much more than having knowledge about him or holding certain theological beliefs. It means *experiencing* in our hearts that God created us for his purpose and that he loves us. We receive a joy which is not dependent upon what we do or who we are, a joy which the world cannot take away because it cannot give it.

Yet I resist this strange joy, even after receiving it. I resist it because of the pain of surrender. It is difficult to admit with St. Augustine that "Thou madest us for thyself, and our heart is restless until it repose in thee." My human nature protests that "Thou madest me for myself, and my heart is restless until I have reached my highest human potential." But slowly, drop by drop, I painfully discover that there is a difference between "my highest human potential" and knowing the only true God. If my highest potential is my goal, then, since I am religious, I try to coopt God as a divine helper. My real interest is not that I experience God, but that I get God to help me achieve my goal of self-fulfillment.

Jesus' goal was radically different. His "food," his purpose for living, was to serve the Father. "Yet not what I want, but what you want." Jesus turns the tables on those who believe that happiness is the goal of human life. For Jesus, happiness is not the goal, but a result of seeking the goal. Only those who are "pure in heart," who seek God above all else, "see" God. If we are willing to lose our lives this way, we will find them. If we endure the pain of putting aside what we think is best and seek God's will first, we slowly discover a strange joy.

However, the battle never ends. Every day we are confronted with choices by which we can seek either ourselves and our immediate desires or God's will. We complain about our jobs and how little we seem to accomplish or how little satisfaction we find in our work. Then slowly and painfully we discover that we have been reversing the process. We have been seeking recognition or personal satisfaction first instead of seeking first to be faithful to the few things which God has set before us. When we are faithful to these few things, a strange joy follows. Strange because it is deep and lasting, not like the fleeting happiness we have been pursuing.

Nowhere is this observation truer than in marriage. When I ask myself whether I am getting as much out of marriage as I put into it, I only feel self-righteous, guilty, or miserable. But when, by the grace of God, I seek my wife's welfare and happiness, even a little, I am overcome by a unique joy. By grace, I forget for a moment whether or not I am giving more than I get. I discover that Jesus was right: "For whoever would save his life will lose it, and whoever loses his life for my sake will find it."

Yet, in other areas I quickly forget Jesus' words and torture myself with questions like whether I am successful or not. Oh yes, I want to do God's will, but I want to do it in a successful way. And *I* will define success in case the Lord wishes to know what it is! Then against my will comes God's awful grace, and I am forced to recognize that I really do not know what is best for me. Especially about how best to use the few years I have left. When I can admit this, and surrender my definition of success, I begin to feel a strange joy—a joy which enables me to work, to create, to achieve, without being completely dependent upon a successful outcome for my efforts.

Every day the struggle arises anew, and every day I suggest a better idea to God. My hope is that he will not listen to me, but help me to listen to my pain and to him. And when I do listen, a special joy creeps in.

This joy is like the satisfaction a musician feels when he or she strikes the perfect chord, even when no one else is listening; or the satisfaction a writer has in turning a good phrase, even if no one else comments on it. We all need recognition, but it is good to know that we can experience joy by simply being in tune with God.

There is also joy in discovering that our disappointments and failures can mature and strengthen us. We still hurt, but are not destroyed by our suffering. It is a great comfort to know that failure does not destroy us, that we have been over that ground before and have survived. Peace and joy come in discovering that setbacks can work for our own good. We are able to ask in the midst of our agony, "What is this experience saying to me? What wisdom can I receive?" Even the ability to ask this question is a sign that wisdom has already come. Then we experience the joy of finding that our suffering was not in vain. A person suffers the humiliation of being arrested for shoplifting; the pain and guilt burn in his consciousness until he realizes that in many other ways he has also been more intent upon getting than giving. The whole painful experience can slowly cause him to reevaluate his life and change its direction.

Some of us have a haunting feeling that our lives are not what they could be. If St. Augustine is right, we can expect only confusion, restlessness, and despair until our hearts find their rest in the One who made us for himself. Millions of people flock to growth weekends promising self-discovery and self-love. Books on how to be OK, how to be your own best friend, and how to look out for #1 are bestsellers. Yet, many of us remain one more weekend or one more book away from salvation. Our appetite is dulled by cotton candy schemes which only increase our malnutrition. Our hunger is assuaged, but our spirits are not fed. Our pain may be temporarily numbed, but actually our hope really lies in our feeling pain again. For the way to the strange joy is always through pain.

This joy is a byproduct of experiencing the acceptance, the trustworthiness, and the pure intent of God. God intends only our salvation, our wholeness, our joy. When we experience that God loves us and accepts us as we are, we experience a joy that is so good it has to be true.

Nothing we could invent or achieve compares with the unique joy of being loved by God. And because we do not earn God's love, we cannot lose it either. God does not abuse us one moment and the next moment pat us on the back. Rather, even in the midst of our pain, he accepts us so much that he suffers with us in order to give us his joy.

As we experience the Hound of Heaven's seeking us through pain, we discover that we can trust such a Pursuer. Our hearts may sink as family and friends fail us at critical moments, but in our pain we discover a love which will not let us go. A strange joy comes over us as we find that we can trust this love without reservation.

We discover that God does not spare us from suffering, but instead goes through the pain with us. Perhaps we were critically ill in the hospital and became sure we were dying. We may have had the sensation that our bed, as well as the room and the entire hospital, was resting on a bog of quicksand. Then as we experienced this sinking feeling, we discovered something else. We sank only so far before we hit bottom. And wonder of wonders, the bottom was solid and it held us. We found rock under us which we could only call "God." Few joys can compare to that joy of discovering that life rests upon solid ground.

A strange joy comes over us as we experience little resurrections in life. One Easter our family had brunch at the Top of the Mark restaurant in San Francisco. I wondered to myself whether or not I had been able to reach the Easter crowd at church that Sunday. Where would they be next Sunday? As everyone else left the table to refill their plates at the buffet, my nineteen-year-old son turned to me and unexpectedly said, "Don't let this go to your head, Dad, but there is no one I respect more than you." I suddenly felt that even if no one showed up at church next Sunday, the joy of my son's remark was resurrection enough.

We can find a strange new joy in marriage. Instead of expecting our partner to make us happy, we may discover that joy which ultimately comes from within ourselves or from God. Our marriage can be resurrected when we no longer ask our partner to *make* us happy. We do not have to demand this when we have received the gift of God's joy. We do not exist for each other's happiness because we have already received an even greater joy. And paradoxically, the less happiness we demand of each other, the more we are able to give to each other. We do not have to be a God-substitute or a joy-substitute for one another. We can enjoy each other and ourselves because we have received a joy which only God can give. The pressure is off us to make each other happy.

The same thing happens with our jobs. As we experience this deep joy, we no longer have to demand that our jobs give us ultimate satisfaction. We can back off from such an unrealistic expectation because our ultimate satisfaction comes from God's love and acceptance. When our work is not expected to be a substitute for God's joy, then we experience little Easters quietly creeping in.

When I approach writing, insisting that what I am is what I write, I feel desperate. Every rejection slip from a publisher is a rejection of my whole being. Then I slowly realize in spite of myself that this isn't so; I am loved and accepted not for what I write, or because of who I am, but simply because I am. As I accept God's love, I experience a strange joy. Then, incidentally, I find that the words come easier.

God has a hidden agenda. He is not content simply to relieve our pain. He passionately desires to give us the joy of knowing the true God and Jesus Christ whom he has sent.

Chapter 2

LISTENING TO THE PAIN

"He's the best physical specimen I've ever seen," our doctor, Frank Williams, observed about our muscular dog, "Satch."

"In that case, Frank, we're going to eat Red Heart and see our veterinarian at least once a year," we told him.

Our kids were frequently reminded never to take Satch outside without a leash. He was too great a threat to cats and joggers, having playfully jumped on the back of one hapless runner. Also, he had no traffic sense and would hurl his powerful body across a busy street at the slightest provocation.

When one of my daughters took him for a run alongside her bike, Satch ran in front of a speeding car and was killed. Our daughter buried him in the backyard.

When my wife and I returned from vacation and heard the news, I took my daughter out and bought a black lab puppy, just like Satch. I wanted to get it before her brother, who took care of Satch, returned home from a camping trip. I could not bear the thought of the pain he would feel. Actually, he took the news quite well; he cried a little, while the cats and joggers breathed easier.

The problem was that I did not realize how instructive and valuable pain can often be. In my desire to silence the pain, I cheated our family of some valuable lessons that pain could teach. We could have shared our feelings and insights surrounding Satch's death which were drowned out by the howls of the new puppy.

For many of us, pain is to be silenced or avoided at all costs. We spend billions of dollars every year on drugs and therapies to rid ourselves of physical and emotional pain. Pain is un-American and unacceptable.

We consider pain to be the opposite of happiness. Not only do we have the right to pursue happiness, but we want to guarantee ourselves and our children the capture of it. And we insist that we and they must be happy *today*. We say that now is the only time there is. We reject the pain of delayed satisfaction.

We also believe that it is good to avoid discomfort at all costs. If people want to stop smoking but conclude that abstinence makes them nervous, we all understand and decide that it is OK for them to smoke. They should not have to feel nervous. The test of the rightness or wrongness of an act is: If it feels good, do it.

When we get ourselves into a distressing situation, we do everything possible to deaden or remove the pain. "Whew! I'm glad that's over." We seldom stop in the midst of the pain, make a friend of it, and allow it to speak to us. We are not geared to thinking of suffering as both necessary and good.

Good pain is pain that teaches us, that pushes our roots deep enough so that we do not have to depend wholly upon the watering of others. Next to love and encouragement, pain is a necessity of growth. Suffering can strip away the frivolous, the excess, the transitory from our lives. We learn, for example, that money or things are a poor substitute for love. In our distress, we discover that transitory possessions do not feed our spirits any more than junk food nourishes our bodies.

We can approach pain as an enemy to be vanquished or as a necessary friend. But pain by itself is not a friend; it is the struggle and change that are occasioned by it that make it a friend. Someone who painfully admits that she has let another person down can grow from this experience. Much of our pain has the possibility of revealing positive insights to us; an accident can teach us much about the pace of our lives; what seems to be a purely physical illness may reveal hidden tensions, guilt, and anger. First it is necessary to admit responsibility and then to suffer the pain of self-revelation.

If we see pain as the archenemy to escape from or to defeat at all costs, then we are hardly prepared to learn from it. All our energy goes into avoiding or fighting suffering. This battle can become a source of despair as we discover the impossibility of eliminating all pain. Too often, the harder we try to eradicate pain, the more it creeps back into our lives. Some of us may try to fight the pain of loneliness by going to a bar and picking up a one-night stand, only to feel more desperately alone the next morning. Or we try to fight growing old and become painfully aware of making fools of ourselves. We take drugs for pain and cloud our minds until we are unable to discover the deeper problem for which pain is a symptom.

In order to grow from suffering it is necessary to change our way of thinking about it even though this runs counter to our culture which insists that *pain is the problem*. Not only does Bufferin advertize that it removes pain, but it removes it faster than Bayer or Anacin. We are dedicated to the notion that pain must be removed as quickly as possible, even before we have heard its message. None of us likes to suffer, and so we try to get out of painful situations as quickly as we can. In a world of instant satisfaction, there has to be instant relief of pain. But in so doing, we escape before we have had the opportunity of learning from our hurt.

There is a critical distinction between being a masochist and being willing to learn from suffering. The masochist gets his reward from the suffering, while the learner gets his reward from the growth he experiences. The masochist suffers because he thinks he deserves it and because he gets a peculiar pleasure from it. The learner does not suffer without asking what the pain is saying to him. Both accept suffering, but for radically different reasons. The masochist believes that pain itself brings pleasure, while the learner believes that pain can reveal the cause of suffering. The masochist accepts pain but not the need to grow from it, while the learner accepts pain in order to grow.

A painless society is a growthless society, but this is not what we like to hear. Adlai Stevenson found that telling the country there were "no gains without pains" was not the way to get elected president. Today, anyone preaching the value of suffering would be regarded as a relic of the Middle Ages or given a psychiatric examination. Suffering simply does not sell.

We teach our children not how to grow from suffering, but how to avoid it. "I do not want my kids to be deprived like I was as a kid." Yet, perhaps not having everything we wanted helped us to grow up. What would happen if, instead of concentrating upon avoiding suffering, we were to help our children deal with suffering creatively? Mike comes home from school and says that if he is late to class again his parents will have to go talk to his counselor. The parents are not eager to do this so plans are put into effect to get Mike out of the house on time. This works as long as the parents get up and push Mike through his morning chores and out the door.

Another approach would be to sit down and ask Mike how he feels about going into school late. If he indicates that he enjoys sleeping in and doesn't mind being late, the parents should let him continue to be late until the situation becomes unbearable. The trouble is it may become unbearable for the parents before it does for Mike. But if Mike says that he really hates being late, there is a beginning for growth. The next question is, "What are you going to do about it, Mike?"

Humans and other animals learn from pleasurable experiences and from painful ones. However, usually we learn more from pain than from pleasure. Pain has a way of shaking us up and causing us to search for new modes of thinking and living in a way that pleasure cannot do. In the midst of gratification we are not likely to ask, "Why is this happening to me?" Yet in painful moments, we are quite apt to ask that question.

We can show our children how to grow from their suffering. The daughter who hears her father complain about the meanness of people where he works soon learns that her father regards his pain as coming from the callousness of others. She would probably grow if she heard her father say, "I got myself into a hassle today which has taught me a good lesson."

One of the chief problems of learning from our pain is that we naturally forget painful experiences as soon as we can. Listen to a group of combat veterans and it sounds as though they had one hilarious exploit after another. They do not talk about dropping napalm on helpless civilians or bayoneting another human being or even about their own wounds. Those things are too painful to remember very long. And since it takes less than a generation to forget these things, we seem to be ready for another war every ten or fifteen years. If every American Legion meeting opened with each member's telling the worst thing he had to do in the war or his most painful experience, it just might be the most resonant chord that could be struck for peace.

The problem of remembering suffering long enough to grow from it is a difficult one. We are simply not prepared to appreciate the value of suffering. Once I had five major operations on my stomach in seven weeks and felt like my body had been donated to medical research. Between operations and during my recovery, I had deep insights about the priorities of my life and the preciousness of time. I failed to write these down, and as I healed the insights faded away. I visited the surgical ward a year later and walked the corridors where once I walked with a pole and an intravenous bottle. But I could not recapture the feeling or the insights.

During my recovery I was preoccupied with getting well, not with what I could learn from the experience. I was so concerned about becoming pain-free that I did not consider that learning from the experience was part of the healing. Without learning what stresses contributed to my illnesses, the healing could hardly be lasting. It was only years later that I gained insight into the self-imposed pressures which contributed to my illness.

At first it seems more painful to take responsibility for our suffering than to blame it upon outside forces. But no one made me sick, and probably no virus attacked me from the outside, or if it did, my own emotional state left me vulnerable to it. The only way to improve my emotional and physical health was painfully to admit my share of the responsibility for illness.

Pain is always a symptom of something else. The time and energy we invest in avoiding this symptom might be more profitably used in grasping its message. Pain is uncomfortable and even unbearable, but it usually is much more than that. The "much more" is discovered only after we cease to make pain *the problem* and get at its cause.

Fortunately, the wound that is causing pain cannot forget, even though we do. So pain continues to fall "drop by drop upon the heart until, in our own despair, against our will, comes wisdom through the awful grace of God." Instead of the absence of grace, pain becomes a means of grace. We discover pain as an untapped resource. Instead of concentrating on eliminating or avoiding it, we can learn how to use it. Pain is seen not as the enemy, but as the symptom of a greater problem.

Still we try to relieve our pain as soon as possible. When the dog is run over, we buy a new puppy immediately. If we are lonely, we seek company, sometimes any company. After a divorce, we may want to find a new partner as quickly as possible. Besides the loneliness, there is a strong need to prove to ourselves and to others that we are still attractive. But in our anxiety to overcome our pain, we may rush into a new relationship which could hurt more than our loneliness. In contrast, the person who allows the pain of divorce to teach new insights about himself or herself has discovered the growth made possible through pain.

By not being willing to endure loneliness, we may rob ourselves of the opportunity of discovering things which can only be learned in solitude. Instead of fighting loneliness, we can accept it as a natural condition and ask what we can learn from it. Then it is possible to move from the pain of loneliness to the satisfying experience of being alone. If we are recently divorced, we can use our single state as a time of assessing what went wrong, what kind of future relationship we may want, or if we want to be married again. But if we fill up our loneliness with distractions and with people who are also afraid to be alone, then we will grow little from our experience. My daughter, Joy, once wrote me a note about her acceptance of aloneness:

> When I experienced this and made a "friend" of heartache, I wasn't afraid of being alone. I then experienced a dramatic growth in my other relation-ships: I had a new appreciation for my old friends who had previously suffered neglect. I had, too, some new-found depths to share. I was made more sensitive to human feelings in general. The key for me was not to *resent* the pain. I think being "spoiled" is when we somehow resent pain as though it shouldn't have happened to us.

When someone says to us, "You must be lonely after your divorce," and we reply, "Yes, sometimes I am, but I need this time to get myself together and to sort out my priorities," then we are listening to our pain.

Chapter 3

AGAINST OUR WILL

Have you had an experience similar to mine in the church service? We come to the confession of sins and read together something like "we are by nature sinful and unclean" or "we have sinned against thee by thought, word, and deed." I look around and wonder whom we are talking about. None of us seems all that bad, and especially not "by nature sinful and unclean." That is such a heavy indictment that few of us will own it. Maybe a gathering of the Mafia or the American Nazi Party should feel this way, but not we respectable church folks who conscienciously do try to live a good life, even a Christian one.

The problem appears to be deeper and more subtle than this. Perhaps the confession that speaks of us all going astray like lost sheep, each one following the devices and desires of his or her own heart, is nearer the truth. Gross sins of the flesh or breaking the Ten Commandments do not fit us as well as the sin of thinking that we have a better way than God does. This means that God has to battle constantly against our wills which in turn always involves pain on his part and ours.

Drop by drop pain falls upon our hearts as our rebellion increases. We think we can end our pain by making wise choices, yet it is our very ability to choose wisely that is impaired. But the more pain we have, the more we depend upon our own mental resources to relieve us. Then when the pain no longer seems bearable, the unexpected happens. We experience what only grace can give: a wisdom and a joy we could not imagine because it did not originate with us. We receive a gift beyond our will.

We feel helpless and despairing that we cannot do anything to end our suffering or to achieve joy. But the other side of this despair is hope. Since the strange joy which comes through grace is not ours to achieve, we are recipients of something we literally could not have dreamed possible. If joy were something to achieve, then it would be limited to what we could learn or squeeze from our pain. Thus, if we had a certain amount of pain, it would be up to each of us to wring as much joy from it as we could.

However, our hope actually lies in the fact that God's joy comes against our will. If we had to agree to accept pain in order to get joy, few of us would endure the effort. Because we often have to be dragged kicking and screaming into joy, there is hope for us. It lies not in the fact that joy comes to us according to our willingness to endure pain, but precisely in an opposite way—joy comes *against* our will. We can rejoice in this since few of us are willing to suffer, even to get joy. If happiness were measured out according to our willingness to suffer, how joyful would any of us become? Conventional wisdom would tell us to get out of such a bargain as quickly as possible.

Instead, God's unconventional wisdom comes through his awful grace. First comes pain, drop by drop, then the unusual and uninvited wisdom of God. Because it is unconventional, our conventional wisdom will always resist it.

The coming of the wisdom of God despite us is good news in a world where everything, for good or evil, seems to depend upon us. God's wisdom comes *not* to those "who help themselves," but to those who *cannot* help themselves. It is the opposite of payment for piecework or working for a commission. Because it involves suffering and pain, it comes against our will. But there is no wisdom or joy from God without suffering.

If we can contribute only our unwilling suffering to the coming of wisdom, how will we find strength to endure our pain? The gospel is the Christian's hope, for in Jesus Christ it demonstrates that God can bring good out of evil, wisdom out of pain, and life out of death. In the gospel we find the hope which enables us to endure our pain because we believe that God can use it for some good. It is difficult to suffer even when we believe that wisdom can come from it; it is unbearable to suffer if we believe that nothing good can come of it.

It may seem encouraging to suggest that God helps

those who help themselves, and that he can accomplish his work if only we humans will cooperate with him. This sounds hopeful until we look at our ingenious ability to foul up any situation, while following what we think is a better way. It is infinitely more helpful to believe that God's wisdom comes despite us.

Suffering and pain are the raw materials God uses to give us his wisdom and joy. With grace, God gives us the confidence that he can bring something unimaginable out of our agony. Without this confidence or faith, we would give up before we received wisdom, or would fail to recognize it when it came.

God uses pain to impart his wisdom, but he does not stop there. When the pain is unbearable and wisdom is slow in coming, God suffers with us. Here the strange wisdom and grace of God reaches its final irony: God does not need suffering in order to grow wise himself, yet he suffers. Perhaps this is the only way he can say that he is sorry we have to suffer in order to become wise. But since he is not able to remove all of our pain, he shares it with us. God does what only the Infinite can do—he suffers infinitely with each of us.

The essence of our sin and rebellion against God lies in thinking that we know better than he does. Many of us have had experiences where we blundered and stumbled along, perhaps for years, before we were willing to admit our error. Sometimes we were even trying to accomplish something we were certain was the will of God. We were too proud to admit that our will was not the same as God's. Maybe it was in our efforts to be "good parents" that we overexerted our will and crossed the line between guiding our children and running their lives. When they rejected our efforts, we confused their rejection of our interference with a rejection of our values. We had to learn painfully that we cannot dominate our children.

We are always growing, always needing more wisdom. In fact, a realization of how unwise and immature we still are is a sign that we have received some wisdom. If we think that we are wise enough to have finally discovered God's will, we should worry. Once we feel we have pinned down his will, we can be certain that we do not know it. God never discloses his wisdom fully, but only "drop by drop" lest we decide to play God, which is as presumptuous as a child who flies a kite and then assumes that he can also fly a 747.

We also need to be wary if we no longer feel pain. If we have anesthetized ourselves to pain, we can hardly learn from it because when we put our hand in a fire the nerves will send no message to the brain. If everything goes too easily and smoothly, we need to ask ourselves if we are still following the Crucified One. Although we do not seek pain or crucifixion, Jesus promised that his followers would share his suffering.

Since we suffer when we try to play God, as well as when we follow him, how do we know the difference? Most likely we never really do know and that is part of our pain. Most of us would be willing to suffer a little if we knew that we were being "fools for Christ." However, when there is a chance that we are suffering simply as "damn fools," we feel another kind of pain. There really is no way we can win, no way to be certain why we suffer. We can only hope that the drop-by-drop wisdom will come even though we fight it.

Although God's wisdom comes against our will, sometimes we find ourselves crying out for it because the pain of living by our own wisdom is unbearable. Our rebellious natures are finally worn down, not because we seek God's will, but because we can no longer bear the pain of living outside of it. Against our wills we finally surrender.

Yet our surrender is never complete. Rather we are like the general who capitulates, but then discovers some fresh troops and an unused cache of arms, so he resumes the battle. When this happens, God can only wait with infinite patience for us to weary of fighting and surrender again. It is critical that God have infinite patience with us because we possess an infinite capacity to seek better ways than his.

Chapter 4

THE GOD WHO SUFFERS WITH US

He grasped my hand in both of his and looked painfully into my eyes. He was an alert eighty-eight-year-old survivor of illnesses that would have finished many younger men. He was attending the funeral of his sister, and at first I thought he was overwhelmed with grief over this loss. He was, but he also suffered an even greater loss. He took me to one corner of the funeral home and explained that his son and daughter were already fighting each other over his estate and "cannot wait until I die." Then his eyes welled up with as much pain as I have ever seen in a human face.

All of us suffer, often daily. We look forward to a reunion with someone close and dear, only to find ourselves saying trivial or even hurtful things, and leaving unsaid the helpful and loving things. Then we suffer remorse for days, possibly weeks and months.

We spend years perfecting our trade or art, and just when we have matured and could make our greatest contribution, we find that younger people are taking our place. No matter how much we rationalize, the hurt stubbornly remains.

We experience physical pain until we wonder if life is worth living anymore. We regain our health, but there is always the fear that the dreaded illness or disease will return. "Arrested," says the doctor, but that does not entirely quiet our anxious mind at 3:00 A.M.

We look at the earth that came from the hand of the Creator, and we know how rapidly we are using up its limited resources and polluting its water and air. We are like TV contestants trying to grab as much as we can in a five-minute dash through the supermarket. When we consider the power of the atom and the madness of the human race, we shudder over what appears to be our fate. We see our children studying hard, planning careers, falling in love, caring for the earth better than we have, and we rejoice. But as we consider the future, we painfully wonder if these children will live long enough to fulfill their potential.

As Christians, we find ourselves unable to think about personal or global suffering without asking where God is in all of this. We know all of the ways to explain or rationalize evil in the world, but we still struggle with one question: "Is God involved in our pain and does he, perhaps, suffer with us?"

Elie Wiesel, who survived the Nazi concentration camp at Auschwitz as a child, later wrote powerful, terrifying books about his memories. He tells of seeing the hanging of another child. As Wiesel watched the death of this child who "had the face of a sad angel," he heard someone behind him groan, "Where is God? Where is he? Where can he be now?" He then heard another voice within himself answer, "Where? Here he is—he has been hanged here, on these gallows."

God really does not answer our haunting questions about the source of evil or how we can square his love with so much suffering in the world. Rather, he lowers himself into the depths of our pain and shares it with us. God does not snatch a child off the gallows, rather he shares the gallows with him. We maybe wish the former, but the latter is what God does.

If we say with Paul that "God was in Christ reconciling the world to himself," we have a handle on suffering. Then Jesus is not the victim needed to satisfy God's sense of justice, but rather God's making himself vulnerable to human caprice. If God cannot remove all suffering, if he is unable to save Jews of all races and classes from the holocaust, then there is only one thing left for a loving and just God to do: Become a Jew himself.

For God to become a Jew or a black or a poor person, or even a rich one, may be too much for us to believe. It requires accepting the idea that God is vulnerable.What if the unthinkable is true, and God depends on us almost as much as we depend on him? What if God still depends upon Judases and Peters like you and me who will either betray him, deny him, or possibly stand by him? Indeed, this is viewing

God from our human perspective. But God may deliberately limit himself in order to share fully in our suffering.

What if Jesus is not simply God playing at being vulnerable for a time by taking a human sabbatical from his heavenly chores? What if Jesus, with his weakness and vulnerability, is what God chooses to be? What if Jesus has revealed what God is doing in every one of us—suffering so that we might possess a strange joy? A joy that can only find us through pain.

What if the cross is not God suffering in Jesus for a moment, like a tragic hero dying on stage only to be resurrected after the curtain goes down, but what if the cross means that God continues to suffer in every one of his daughters and sons? What if God in Jesus didn't simply die "once and for all" for our sins, but suffers and dies with each one of us? What if God is the Eternal Parent suffering with each of his sons and daughters, dying countless deaths with them each day? What if God's unlimitedness means that he suffers unlimited pain? What if God's greatness is measured by the greatness of his suffering? What if he can actually feel pain as much as we do? Then God is not the plantation owner sipping a mint julep on his heavenly porch while the slave driver beats and kills the slaves in the fields. Rather, God himself is a slave.

This is not the can-do-anything, "How Great Thou Art" God we have been raised with. At first it is frightening and appalling to think of God's continuous pain. Later it is hopeful. Our vulnerable Father is not

unmoved by his children's pain. Quite the opposite—
our pain becomes his pain. God! Do you really feel all
the pain suffered by every one of your children?

It is impossible to talk about suffering without
talking about risking. There is no suffering which does
not also involve the pain of uncertainty. We could
suffer much if we only knew that everything would
turn out all right in the end. We could endure walking
across a burning desert if we knew there would be a
cold well on the other side.

God suffers in a way which only God can suffer. He
has purposely chosen to limit his power and thus has to
endure the agony of being all-powerful, yet "unable" to
right every wrong or remove every pain.

The suffering of God can be explored on two levels.
One is the suffering of God as Father and the other is his
suffering as Son. Christianity has long used these
metaphors to talk about God. However, God's suffering is more than metaphoric; it is actualized in Jesus and
in all human suffering.

God suffers like any father who sees great hopes
for his children shattered. God sent his son to save us
from our wrongheadedness and pride, only to see that
these very qualities in us crucified Jesus. When God
sent Jesus into the world, he was like any father seeing
his son off on a promising career or a life-saving
mission. God had high hopes for his son and for his
reception in the world. Surely people who had long
stumbled in darkness would rejoice to see the Light.

Think of how you or I would feel after investing

thirty years and more than a hundred thousand dollars in raising and educating a gifted child. Then suppose this child graduated from medical school and dedicated herself to working among the poor in an urban ghetto. Then suppose someone brought a false malpractice suit against her, and suppose other people spread rumors that she was a quack, and that soon after someone burned down her office and destroyed her equipment. Finally, suppose the people she had come to help were tricked, and that a few community leaders took her to a shopping center and shot her in cold blood. Wouldn't our parental grief be without limit and beyond comfort?

Now try to think the unthinkable: Suppose we had other children at home and that one by one we saw the same thing happen to them. It is beyond human capacity to comprehend the suffering of seeing child after child crushed and brutalized in this way. But suppose that God continues to suffer with us as his son is crucified six million times in Nazi ovens, burned by napalm, starved, and beaten. Can God, who by definition is not subject to our human frailties, feel pain? Can God let himself feel what it is impossible for him to feel? This is like the old question of whether God can make a stone too heavy for him to pick up.

What if God's power lies not in remaining beyond our suffering, but in choosing to share it with us? Suppose God's power is the power to bridge the gulf between the divine and the human and to do what any self-indulgent god does not do. If five-star generals won't crouch in foxholes, then what business does God have suffering? But suppose he does suffer just as each of us does, only multiplied by the number of people on earth. Then God's power lies not in his ability to escape suffering, but in his willingness to share it. We humans measure power by our capacity to avoid pain, but God's power lies in his choosing to be vulnerable. For us "rank has its privilege"; for God rank means that he is the first to suffer.

God is not subject to our human weakness, but supposing he refuses to abide by all rules and regulations agreed upon by theologians. If this is the way God works, we have a kind of rogue elephant God who does what he blessed well pleases.

If God suffers like we do, only infinitely, then how can he be more powerful than pain or evil? It would seem that the power of evil has the final say about God. But again, we come to the "my ways are not your ways" kind of God. God simply does not do us the courtesy of operating according to our logic. Instead, he becomes subject to pain in order to overcome it.

In Jesus, God did what cannot be done. He suffered as a human being. If he did this once on a suffering sabbatical, we might understand it. But what if God continues to suffer through countless others of his children? Through suffering we are all made sons and daughters of God, as Paul contends, "we are children of God, and if children, then heirs, heirs of God and fellow heirs with Christ, provided we suffer with him in order that we may also be glorified with him."

Christ must still be suffering in order for us, who are presently alive, to suffer with him. Paul speaks of completing the suffering of Jesus in our own bodies. God's battle with pain is not over, nor is it fully won. The first returns have appeared with Jesus, but the final count is still coming in. God is more powerful than evil in the sense that he is willing to suffer what he could avoid. Evil would have final power over God if he were to refuse to suffer. It is God's willingness to suffer that reveals that his love is greater than the power of evil.

Obviously, we cannot know for sure that God really feels rejection, despair, and failure. Many would argue that this is too human and anthropomorphic an idea of God. Perhaps so, but does not being God mean that God is not bound by any preconceptions we would put on him? God does not have to behave as God is supposed to act. If he chooses to overcome evil by suffering it, that is his business. He can be an involved and vulnerable God if he wishes, instead of a Retired Chairman of the Board.

The thought that God suffers the same pain as each of us does, only multiplied by all the people who have ever lived, is an unthinkable thought. But only God can hold the paradox together; only God can do what cannot be done.

Finally, God hears our hurt because it is his own hurt. When Jesus was rejected it was not simply a matter of a good man being put down. It was our way of putting God down. It was our way of saying to God that we have a better idea. It was each of us singing, "I did it my way." In Jesus, God suffered that we might see the Light and come to our senses, or at least begin to question our own wisdom. How must God have felt when he saw that all his suffering was to no apparent avail? When God saw his son being rejected, he knew that he also was being rejected, as has been the case since Eden.

God had a baby son so that we might know how sacred human life is to him. Although a handful of shepherds and three traveling seers rejoiced, King Herod threw a paranoid rage and ordered all Bethlehem infants under two years of age killed. God came with a message of "peace on earth, goodwill to all people" and was greeted with the slaughter of the innocents. How must God, the new Father, have felt seeing the agony of other parents as their children were murdered?

Instead of thinking that God has unlimited power, we might consider that he has an unlimited capacity to suffer. God's long-promised Messiah was born in a barn, the child of a poor girl. Had she applied for Aid to Dependent Children, the rich who are busy avoiding taxes would have complained bitterly. Did Jesus learn as a child that his birth had occasioned the deaths of hundreds of other children? If so, he discovered early the same suffering which was in store for him. What a sinking feeling he must have felt in the pit of his stomach when he realized that pure love is so misunderstood and rejected.

As a curious twelve-year-old discussing theology

and philosophy with his elders, Jesus began to feel that he was destined for a special role. As a devout young Jew, he could feel that God's hand was leading him. Jesus had high hopes for the success of his work, like any ambitious young man starting his career. In good faith he asked people to join him in a venture which he believed would accomplish much to the glory of God. When things went otherwise, Jesus had to cope not only with his own despair, but that of his friends as well. It is one thing to admit failure to oneself, and another to tell people that the cause you recruited them for has gone sour.

Think of impetuous Peter, full of life, tired of the old ways, willing to risk. He senses in the Galilean someone who knows who he is and why he is. No extravagant offers are made, no money changes hands; quite the contrary, Peter is challenged to leave all and follow this man. He does and his friends hide their amusement and skepticism. "You mean that all he said to you was, 'Follow me and I will make you fishers of men?' Who is he, anyway, Peter? How do you know he isn't just another crazy prophet? How do you know?" When Peter came home and told his wife what he was going to do, the response was anguishing, "You mean you are going to leave me for some wandering rabbi who has no following and no money? How can you do this to me? If you were running off with another woman it would kill me, but to run after this fellow makes me sad for you, Peter. Sad for both of us. How can you do it, Peter?"

He hurried away in the night to join his rabbi,

hurried away so he wouldn't have to answer any more questions. As he passed the Sea of Galilee he glanced back at the shimmering waters, at his boat and nets, back at the good life of a fisherman. Now he was to catch—catch men! What in the name of God did that mean? Maybe his wife and his friends were right after all.

And there are those strange words about turning your cheek, giving your cloak, loving your enemies. Enigmatic sayings about wolves in sheep's clothing and not gathering figs from thistles. There is also the healing of the military officer's son and Peter's mother-in-law. But as soon as he gains a little respectability, what does this rabbi up and do? He drives demons into a herd of swine and the latter rush over a cliff to their death! What to tell the owner of the swine? Think fast, Peter.

On and up the twisting trail. Hang on, Peter. One minute this rabbi has the crowd cheering and the next chasing him with rocks. First he has the religious establishment spellbound, now he is calling them hypocrites and whitewashed tombs. What have you gotten yourself into, Peter? Go back and tell your wife it was all a mistake. Are you following him only because you're afraid to admit you were wrong?

The twelve all suffered in silence for a time. As things began to fall apart, they tried to rescue their teacher from his dream. Peter suggested that they stay on the mountain top with their visions, until things cooled off. But Jesus was bent on something none of them could comprehend. They wondered whether even he knew. They were engulfed in despair, the worse because they could not identify it, much less head it off. Jesus read their expressions. First confusion, then doubt, then anger began to creep in around the edges of their faces and soon they couldn't look at him any longer. Yes, they deserted him, but didn't he first desert them? When Peter swore that he did not know him, he spoke the truth. He did not know this man, once young and bold, now haunted and old. Once all hope and promise, now all pain and despair. Small wonder Peter did not know him. Their dreams and hopes were gone; all that remained was the awful smell of failure and death.

Forsaken by friends who themselves felt forsaken, Jesus must still face the pain—God, the pain—of his mother. How could he comfort her when it was he who had brought her here?

All hope is gone, save one. And that hope is the incredible claim that God is not looking at this terrible event from a distant heaven. God does not run away with the rest of them. There on the cross all the pain of heaven and earth are focused. And Jesus feels deserted and cries out to God in his abandonment.

Then a strange thing takes place. God answers the painful cry "My God, my God, why hast thou forsaken me?" through the lips of a dying thief. A criminal asks Jesus for mercy, but only after extending to him the ultimate therapy of identifying his pain with Jesus' pain. In his last moments, Jesus was comforted by a man who also needed comfort. It was not the blind leading the blind, but the dying comforting the dying. God did not abandon his son on the cross, rather he came to him in the guise of another son dying on the next cross.

It is not those who are untouched by suffering, but those who are all but broken by it who can minister to each other. The poignancy of pain becomes its power. Only when deep speaks to deep, and pain speaks to pain, can we be healed and comforted. God does not abandon us, for he gives us each other.

Chapter 5

BORN AGAIN EVERY DAY

Richard Niebuhr, a theologian's theologian, was walking with a colleague near the Yale campus when he was stopped by an earnest young evangelist who inquired, "Are you saved?" Niebuhr thoughtfully replied, "Yes." The inquirer pressed, "When?" Niebuhr replied, "Every day."

If we only emphasize rebirth at a special time and place, we can forget that the process of pain and rebirth goes on all our lives. We are saved every day. It was *after* the apostle Paul was born again on the road to Damascus that he anguished, "For I do not do the good I want, but the evil I do not want is what I do."

Martin Luther experienced the same thing after discovering that his salvation was a gift, and not something he could earn. He believed that baptism was more than a single event in our lives. He said that the "old Adam" in us needed to be "drowned and destroyed by daily sorrow and repentance" and that a "new man should daily come forth."

Rebirth for Paul and Luther meant a continuous

dying to the old and being born to the new. Once you feel that you have it made, that the struggle is over, watch out. It is like Jesus' parable of the seven spirits who repossessed an unwary victim when he felt he had his house in order, "and the last state of that man becomes worse than the first."

Instead of being saved in sterile Saran Wrap, we become aware of our daily need for repentance and renewal. That is why Jesus left us the Holy Spirit, a continuous source of power, rather than a static formula. We are saved every day and that means pain. In fact, God often uses pain to remind us that we cannot be smug about our rebirth. Paul talked about his visions and revelations, but said "a thorn was given me in the flesh, a messenger of Satan, to harass me, to keep me from being too elated." He said that he asked the Lord three times to take away the thorn, but the Lord said to him, "My grace is sufficient for you, for my power is made perfect in weakness."

God works despite, even because of, our weakness and pain. A painless rebirth is as impossible as a painless birth. *Not all pain results in growth, but all growth results in pain.*

People who can point to their rebirth at a definite time and place have the same problem of pain and struggle as those for whom salvation is a daily process. In fact the significance of a time and place is that this was when we first became conscious of the Spirit working in us. That was the Spirit pouring the footings for a building which will take all our lives to build.

We all suffer pain, but rebirth means that we know how to use our pain creatively. We no longer have the pain of feeling that our suffering is futile. We can receive most pain as a resource to be used for our good. For the reborn there is little wasted pain. Most pain, even pain we would gladly refuse, can be used for some good. This does not mean that we go out of our way to seek pain; there is always plenty of it around seeking us. But it does mean that we never let pain slip through our fingers and suffer, literally, for the hell of it. We suffer for our redemption, for our growth in grace.

Birth is painful, but so is growing up. No one would say that being born is enough; in fact it is only the beginning. We cannot remember the time and place when we were first born, but we can recall where we were today, what we said or did not say, what we did or did not do. We can recall painful experiences from the distant and the near past. We can ask what these experiences tell us about ourselves. Like Paul and his thorn, we can discover that God's power is made perfect in our weakness and in our pain.

It is the reborn who can say that pain is not wasted. Rebirth is the ability to see and to use suffering in a new way. If Paul were not reborn, the thorn in his flesh would simply be painful; instead it became a "messenger," something "to harass me, to keep me from becoming too elated." *The converted are those who know how to convert pain from a nuisance to a reminder.*

But what about people who have far more pain than is needed to remind them? Does not too much pain break, rather than make, people? We know this is true and we pray that God will not test us with more pain than we can handle. We pray "deliver us from evil." It is important not to see God as the cause of all pain, since he is not in the business of breaking people. Rather, by suffering with us, God hallows our struggle to learn from pain. When pain threatens to break us, we can only cry out as Jesus did on the cross, "Father, into thy hands I commit my spirit!" We have hope because we commit our spirits into the hands of a suffering God who understands, not an idle spectator.

For those not reborn, pain must be avoided at all costs. It is a negative that must be minimized. However, a sign of rebirth is when we look at pain in a new way. We do not invite pain into our lives, but when it comes, we pay attention to it. All people suffer; those who are born again know how to listen to their pain.

Being reborn daily means a new and ever-growing appreciation of one's life, even one's anguish. Life is seen as the Way, the journey with, and to, God. Most suffering can teach us something, even though some of it is unexplainable. The reborn person does not always understand pain, but is aware of the untapped resources in it.

Just as birth is painful, so is rebirth. Before we can be reborn we must die. We must die to pride and ambition which insists that we know what is best for us. This dying to ourselves is one of the most painful experiences in life. It is impossible to so die except for the awful grace of God. However, after we experience living for ourselves, we become less resistant to dying to ourselves. When ourselves become too great a burden to carry, we cry out for the grace we need to die to our pride.

Dying and being born again is not all pain. Wisdom comes as we relax our frantic grip on life and "let God be God." This wisdom, through "the awful grace of God," brings with it a strange kind of joy. Not a joy without pain, but a joy which can face the torment and even say, "What more can you do to me?" It is a joy that exists despite, and even because of, the pain. It has been forged and tempered in suffering. It is a joy or peace which passes understanding because it has moved past understanding to trust. It is a joy which says about pain, "I don't like it, but I have been there before. It cannot separate me from the love of God, a love which suffers with me."

After being reborn, we are not spared pain, but we are spared hopelessness. We are spared the feeling that God is absent or indifferent while we suffer. We know better than to think that pain serves no earthly purpose. We are not left with the desperate feeling that suffering and death are more powerful than God. We have, drop by drop, experienced the opposite.

Chapter 6

WHO GRADES OUR PAPERS?

A thirty-fifth high school class reunion is a good time to observe the mid-life crisis. By the time we are fifty most of the dreams of our youth have been reached, shattered, or discarded. For some people there is a growing acceptance that life is good without reaching the stars. For others there is a bitter resignation that they will never reach their full potential.

Whatever the outlook of the participants, the reunion games go on. The same old conversations, the same old jockeying for position. In one corner the class conservative trades blows with the class liberal; neither has changed his mind in thirty-five years. The faded class flirt is still hustling, now with the aid of a few gin and tonics. The jocks are bald and paunchy, except for the one former benchwarmer who looks like he could now make the team. The lawyer, who was thrown out of law school for giving test answers to a classmate, but was later allowed to reenter, has to explain to everyone what happened over thirty years ago. The surprise of the evening is the "ugly duckling," one of those plump girls who had a locker near yours, who now looks like a homecoming queen at fifty-two.

Who grades the papers? Who has "passed" and who has "flunked"? Some people come to the class reunion expecting to be graded by the rest of the class. A few may feel that the class reunion grade means more than their school grades did. Others will wake up with a hangover and wish they had not played the game at all.

Many of us experience a "passed over" feeling by fifty. We have seen some of our friends make it to the top and then topple, much to our delight. But as our smile fades, we are alone with our thoughts. Will we ever go any further than we have gone now? Then sometimes we wonder if we really do know which way is "up." There is still an agreed upon direction for success which most of us share, at least until we think more about it. Some of us may not prize money for itself, rather it may be power or fame or influence that we seek. Who of us, except someone half dead, does not want to leave more of an impression on the world than a fist does after being removed from a bucket of water?

But realistically, what can we expect after fifty? If we are not too different inside from that face in the yearbook, then how much can we expect to change in the next twenty-five years? The pain of feeling passed over causes many to crowd the bar at the class reunion. It is good not to skip through the anguish too quickly.

The pain can be a catalyst to help us consider what we really want out of life.

Most of us like to believe that pain and stress are the result of modern living. We complain that the pace is too hectic, and we long for a quieter time and place. To be sure, outside pressures do create stress, but not all of it. Some of us have discovered that we create much of our stress inside of ourselves. We carry instant stress around with us, and it takes little or no outside pressure to activate it. We can go on vacation to a peaceful lake and feel anxious just thinking about something back home we had done or not done.

If much of our pain and stress comes from within, then there should be something we can do about it. Freud and others have held that if we could only get back to the origin of our anxiety, we could eliminate or at least deal with it. But many people have found that discovering the origin of anxiety, if indeed they really could, is not enough. There has to be more than understanding; we need some kind of leverage on the problem.

It helps to recognize that we often create our anxiety by expecting too much of ourselves. We live beyond our ability to fulfill our dreams and beyond life's ability to fulfill them. It is the distance between where we are and where we think we should be which often causes anxiety. Someone will quickly add that if we did not have goals, even impossible dreams, the human race would stagnate. Goals and dreams are essential, but discontent and a gnawing feeling of failure are quite different.

We ask ourselves, "What makes life worth living?" or "How do we know when we have succeeded?" Some people suggest that success is not in our achievement but in our struggle. But is there also some time when we can relax, feeling we have done all we can, and that the rest is up to God or fate or both? We don't mean to be complacent, certainly not apathetic, but confident that if our work is done to the glory of God, he will find a way to use it.

It is interesting to note that the word "success" never appears in the Bible. There are parables and other references to being faithful stewards or being found faithful, but not to being successful. Apparently the latter is not ours to determine.

The acceptance of the biblical criterion of success can free us from much of the anxiety we have over whether we have made it or not. The Word suggests that we will never know anyway, and that there can be peace in the acceptance of this fact. The Word teaches that, although we might not succeed in our work, we can succeed as a person. If true success cannot be determined by us and is measured only by God, then it would seem useless to strain for worldly success.

The old doctrine of justification by faith has narrowly meant that we cannot earn our way into heaven by good works, that we enter it only by the grace of God. (Paul Holmer of Yale Divinity School says that he frequently hears pastors warning their flocks of the futility of working their way into heaven. But when he looks around the parish, he notes that few are even trying to do so.) Finding an accepting God and gaining heaven instead of hell was a problem for Martin Luther, but we seldom ask the question in this fashion today. Rather we are likely to wonder, "How do I know when I have made it here on earth?" or "Who grades my paper?"

Once people lived in dread that God would measure them and find them wanting. Now we live in dread that other people, and we ourselves, will measure us and find us wanting. Our anxiety and suffering have no end because we can never know if we are acceptable in the eyes of other people. Since we are usually harder on ourselves than others are on us, we will also be unsure whether or not we have ever made it in our own eyes. Since all human judgments are fallible, our only hope is to be measured by Someone related to, but also outside of, our human family.

The strange story of God's becoming man is so incredible that it just might be the answer to our dilemma. It is claimed that Jesus was one of us, but also more than one of us. If he really represents God to us and us to God, then maybe we have a new insight into the problems of success and failure. Because Jesus was not successful in the ways we measure success, God's yardstick reads differently from ours. If Jesus is really God's hidden success story, then we might as well give up on trying to measure success. God simply will not play by our rules.

If we believe that God's definition of success is what really counts, should we give up striving for any form of success on earth—material, social, or spiritual? Not at all. But being justified by faith or saved by grace means that we can now minimize the pain and anxiety over whether we are successful or not. We can devote our energies to our work, to the various tasks God has called us to without worrying about a heavenly or an earthly box score. By accepting and loving us as we are, Jesus frees us from the anxiety of having to prove ourselves to ourselves or to our classmates at the thirty-fifth class reunion.

We are graded by God's grace which does not include our ways of measuring success. And since we cannot earn his approval, we can only accept it gratefully. We are then free to achieve and to create without the crippling compulsion that the works of our hands must validate our lives. We are already valid, so now we can get on with living.

Chapter 7

THE PAINFUL JOY OF SURRENDER

Frank Sinatra's theme song is "I did it my way." Most of us probably do not agree with Frank's way, but we can appreciate the feeling of independence and individuality behind the song.

"Ford has a better idea" makes good mechanical and advertising sense, but it raises questions in theology. In fact, the origin of sin in the old Garden of Eden story involves Adam and Eve's suggesting to the Lord that they had "a better idea." History is replete with similar examples.

Faith in God means that we trust that he has a purpose for our lives. God is not like a puppy standing on the street corner wagging his tail and begging every passerby to take him home. God works with infinite patience and love first to plant the seed, then to carefully water and nurture it in hopes that it will bear fruit. He is willing to create a million seeds with the hope that one will grow.

Many of us constantly have to struggle against the temptation to play God or to suggest to God what is best for us. Then, after many falls and bruises, we reluctantly come to accept the awful grace of God. This awe-full grace comes to us when we painfully learn the folly of trying to play God, to be captains of our own souls. We finally surrender to God because it is too painful to do anything else.

> In our sleep, pain which
> cannot forget, falls drop by drop
> upon the heart until, in our own despair,
> against our will, comes wisdom through
> the awful grace of God.

Surrendering to God is not like General Robert E. Lee's offering his sword to General Ulysses S. Grant. Rather it is a process of becoming free by being a captive. "Force me to render up my sword, and I will conqueror be," wrote hymn writer George Matheson. There is pain and suffering involved in·doing this, but not the self-destructive pain of assuming that we know best. It hurts our pride to admit that we do not know what is best for ourselves, much less for other people. But this admission can lead to a new and amazing freedom.

When we find our freedom in captivity to God, we no longer have to suffer the burden of proving our worth to ourselves or to other people. We admit that any such proof is hardly conclusive and easily demolished by contrary opinions. It is a freeing experience to settle back and say, "God alone is capable of judging my life, and he alone knows the best way it can be used."

Some people may see this as a resignation that robs

us of our humanity, we become puppets, albeit God's puppets. But God does not function as we do. If a person gave him or herself to another in this way, the human tendency would be for one to dominate the other. *Strangely, the more of ourselves we surrender to God, the more of ourselves he gives back to us.*

God is the wise parent because he constantly encourages us to stand on our own feet. We pray that God will help us mend a broken relationship with someone. Then we become aware not of what God will do, but of what we ourselves can do. The more we pray for help, the more God reveals to us that we are not helpless. God surely helps us, but in a way that increases, rather than decreases, our responsibility. When we seek God's guidance rather than our own way, we become most profoundly ourselves.

Just as a person grows wise by admitting the limits of his or her own knowledge, so also a person becomes free by accepting limits to personal desires and ambitions. We are like rivers who find their power and destiny by flowing between banks rather than flowing everywhere. There is creative pain in seeking God's will, unlike the destructive pain of denying it.

The difference between rendering up our sword and thinking we have is often unclear, especially to ourselves because of our infinite capacity for self-deception. Perhaps the way we can know that we have really surrendered is when we are willing to suffer the pain of canceled dreams. Can we accept the fact that someone else, not we, received the promotion, and ask,

"If not this, what do you have for me to do, Lord?" and then be willing to await and pursue further orders without complaint or bitterness?

We can also listen to our pain. Do we suffer because we did not get what we want? To be sure, this is frequently the case. But is our suffering also because we sense that we have been working counter to God's purposes and yearn to work with them instead? The pain of bending our wills to God is different from the pain of trying to bend God's will to ours. A wild horse is easy to break compared to attempting to tame God. Jesus' final, awful struggle in Gethsemane was over whether he would follow his or God's will.

Trusting God can be both painful and joyful. It is always painful to surrender our autonomy, but it can also lead to a strange joy. A joy that is only known to those who find their lives by losing them. "Let us run with perseverance the race that is set before us, looking to Jesus the pioneer and perfecter of our faith, who for the joy that was set before him endured the cross, . . ." Obviously, the joy came not in the cross, but in being faithful to God's will, to the mission God gave him to accomplish. Joy is most likely to come to us as a consequence of being faithful.

Listen to the pain. Where does it come from? What is it saying? What disappointments, longings, heartfelt desires is it reflecting? Emotional pain, like its twin, physical pain, is a symptom of something else. Is it that we cannot manipulate God and the world around us to our own liking? Or is it that pain is falling drop by drop, upon our heart until, in our own despair, against our will, wisdom is coming through the awful grace of God?

Finally we painfully learn that we cannot use God, but can only be used by him. We may have enlisted in his ranks, but we continue to march off on our own. We are weary and footsore from stumbling on our paths. But when we surrender ourselves to him, we discover the strange joy of finding ourselves. Once we stop demanding that God follow our paths, we are free for the joy and adventure of his way because the more of ourselves we surrender, the more of us we get back.

Chapter 8

THE JOY OF FORGIVENESS

Some of us carry instant guilt which can be activated by a word or a glance. Feeling guilty is a way of life for some of us. We spend much time and energy regretting foolish things we have said or done or, worse yet, feeling guilty over things we cannot identify. A cartoon showed a cluster of inmates in a prison yard looking at another prisoner walking with his head bowed low. One in the cluster says to the others, "What I can't stand about that guy is his guiltier-than-thou attitude."

We may go to church every Sunday and hear that we are forgiven without these words soaking into our parched souls. It does little good to blame our parents who may have manipulated us with guilt. The question is what are we going to do now about feeling guilty. Until we can be free of this destructive pain, we waste much of our energy and suffer unproductively.

It is helpful to distinguish between being guilty and feeling guilty; it is the latter which is often futile and sick. For example, some of us white people feel guilty about the way blacks and other minorities have been and still are oppressed. But as long as we are simply reacting to past injustices we can hardly do very much about present inequities. For guilt to be productive, it must be focused upon actual incidents which we can do something about. Otherwise we only wallow around in our bad feelings.

Guilt feelings do not produce growth in us. Quite the opposite. We either turn the guilt in upon ourselves and often become literally sick, or we turn the feeling outward and become angry. It is no surprise that many racists have grown up with the effects of racism before their eyes. They have seen blacks or Jews or Indians suffer outrageously, but instead of a healthy guilt which works for an end to oppression, they develop sick guilt feelings and find "reasons" why the oppressed should suffer. The Ku Klux Klaners and Nazis handle their guilt feelings by increasing their hatred and persecution.

People who deal with guilt in a sick fashion cannot accept or give forgiveness. They seek to subdue their sick guilt by telling themselves they have nothing to feel guilty about. Then as their guilt boils inside of them, they strike out in rage against those who make them feel guilty. Asking a Nazi Storm Trooper or a guard at Dachau if he feels guilty misses the point. Of course he will say that he doesn't; the Jews brought it all on themselves. Unacknowledged and unforgiven guilt can only continue to bring suffering to the holder of it and to those people it is projected upon.

Richard Nixon is a classic example of a man bearing uncreative and sick suffering. As long as he cannot acknowledge responsibility for Watergate, he will continue to suffer. He is in an escape-proof prison with himself as the eternally vigilant guard. His suffering leads to nowhere except to more suffering. On the other hand, he could have gone on television and said, "I accept full responsibility for Watergate. I am ready to submit to any further penalty there may be. I apologize to the American people, and I ask your forgiveness." He could know that God has forgiven him, his family has forgiven him, and he could forgive himself. He could know a strange joy and peace.

The pain of unrelieved guilt, particularly when we will not forgive ourselves, is often the greatest source of suffering there is. Like St. Paul, some of us feel chained to a corpse of guilt. We cry out for freedom from this "body of death," but we are not quite willing to cut the deadly bonds. Then we find to our joy that what we cannot do for ourselves, God through Jesus Christ does for us.

It is not necessary to delve into long, analytical explanations of why we refuse to let go of our guilt. We know about masochism and the need to suffer; we have heard Freudian explanations of why we do not forgive ourselves. But explanations are not helpful because they only lead to reasons and we need to find release.

Guilt is an essential part of growth. We usually do not change our way of doing things until we feel guilty or uneasy about our present actions. However, if we hold on to our guilt instead of accepting forgiveness, we do not learn from it. Rather, the opposite takes place; we can become immobilized by guilt and arrested in growth. After guilt has awakened in us a need for forgiveness and change, we can either accept these or, like Mr. Nixon, we can wallow in guilt. When we accept forgiveness and let go of our guilt, we grow.

Like the many explanations of why we hold on to guilt, there are various alternatives for dealing with guilt. We can incant "I'm OK—You're OK." We can rationalize that we are no better or worse than the rest of the human race, but feelings cannot be squelched by such rational attacks. The Christian alternative to guilt is sternly simple; it is like a "narrow gate" through which all must pass who seek a godly answer to the human problem of guilt. It is narrow because few of us want to take responsibility for our lives. It is much easier to blame our problems on a messed up childhood or upon temptations that are too great for the flesh. As long as Richard Nixon insists that he was fooled by his friends and betrayed by his enemies, he cannot discover the strange joy of being forgiven. He has been legally pardoned, but has not been released from his pain or his prison.

Those who find and enter the narrow gate are those who are willing to face up to the cause of their guilt. "It's not the preacher, not the deacon, but it's me, O Lord, standin' in the need of prayer." This lyric sounds quaint, smacks of the sawdust trail, and its very simplicity offends the worldly wise. Yet those who are wise in another sense find release and comfort in confession to God.

Guilt is like the starter in an automobile—necessary for getting the engine going, but if we drive on the starter, we are soon in trouble. Guilt is useful as a sign that something is wrong, but it is destructive as a long-term motivation, and the needless suffering it produces is immeasurable.

Although the church with its gospel of forgiveness should be most helpful in the alleviation of guilt, it has not always been so. In fact, it has frequently increased rather than decreased people's guilt. The church too often sees itself primarily as the *guardian* of moral law, rather than as the *proclaimer* of grace. Thus, people often leave the church after a divorce instead of finding forgiveness and joy in an accepting community.

It is debatable whether conviction of guilt is indispensible to change. Sometimes we are inspired to change our lives when our sins and shortcomings are pointed out to us. More likely, however, we are apt to change when we see godliness and goodness in people who inspire us to be more than we are. The pangs we experience when we realize that we could be using our lives better is different from gnawing guilt or the feeling of unworthiness. The former experience is positive since it says that we are more capable than we think, whereas feeling unworthy is a paralyzing experience that suggests we can never change.

The greatest boon to humankind would be a way of dramatically declaring that God loves us as we are, and because he does, we can become what we are not yet. This is precisely what the cross and the gospel are all about. Jesus came to rid us of our guilt feelings and to help us deal creatively with our guilt. About our guilt feelings he says, "Father, forgive them for they know not what they do." About our guilt he says, "Go, and sin no more."

Guilt for Jews and Christians is a theological problem, and a necessary, but not a permanent, state. King David ordered a man killed so he could have his wife. When he accepted responsibility for his sin, he cried to God, "Against thee, thee only, have I sinned, and done that which is evil in thy sight, so that thou art justified in thy sentence and blameless in thy judgment."

There can be no lasting forgiveness without a Forgiver, no self-acceptance without divine acceptance. Rationalizing or psychoanalyzing guilt is like painting over rust. There must first be a rust remover. We cannot just rush in and paint Jesus' name over our corroded lives.

Before we experience the peace of forgiveness we experience the pain of repentance. Terribly old-fashioned words, but which of the new ones reach as deeply into our lives to remove the rust? St. Paul knew the pain that comes before the peace, "Miserable creature that I am, who is there to rescue me out of this body doomed to death? God alone, through Jesus Christ our Lord! Thanks be to God!"

The unbearable pain which King David, St. Paul,

and President Nixon all experienced can lead to the unimagined peace and the strange joy of divine forgiveness. David's acceptable sacrifice of "a broken spirit; a broken and contrite heart" is also answered in a vision of forgiveness found in Isaiah, "And he touched my mouth, and said: 'Behold, this has touched your lips; your guilt is taken away, and your sin forgiven.' "

As we die to ourselves before we are reborn, so we acknowledge our sin and pride before we are free. Such death is an admission of our human limitations, just as confession is a shattering of our pretenses. When these prisons of pretense and guilt are shattered, we walk in freedom and joy.

Chapter 9

A LAUNCHING PAD

He was a good father, perhaps too good. He has made a career of parenting, and now his career is over, or at least radically changed. It has ended too soon for him, but none too soon for his children.

It is painful to stop playing the wise father, particularly when he enjoyed his work. In what other field does a man have to retire just as he has reached the zenith of his proficiency? All the years of trial and error, of learning and listening, that go into being a father now must be forgotten. Just as he grasps what the job is all about, he has to resign. The best use he can put to his skills as a wise and patient counselor is to stop using these skills. It is like asking a struggling artist to stop painting just as he gains recognition.

The faith required to let go of a son or daughter makes removing a mountain look like a simple task. The mountain or role of parenting, particularly that of a good parent, is difficult to remove. But it must go, otherwise the son or daughter will be buried by it.

The father has made mistakes, but he has grown

from them. He has served a painful apprenticeship, but now he can no longer practice his trade. He realizes that his very skills as a parent are working against his child. A child must break loose, rebel, cut the cord. This task may be easier if the parent is cruel or lacks understanding. It is not easy if a child must break with a kind, patient, and loving parent. And habits, particularly those which bring satisfaction, are difficult to break. It isn't that the father wants to block a daughter's growth or make her forever dependent upon him. It simply is rewarding for him to have his daughter seek him out for company and advice. None of his associates at work regard him with such esteem but he can look upon his parenting job and say, "When all is said and done, I know that I have been a good father." Then a painful voice from within whispers, "Yes, but quit while you're ahead."

The fact that his paid vocation has reached a plateau increases the pain of ending his career as a father. He knows that he will never be more than a district sales manager with the company. The dream of becoming president of the firm, or even vice-president in charge of sales, has vanished. Already a younger man holds the latter job, and there are several ahead of him for the presidency. Then he discovers that he can still be "president" in his daughter's eyes. As he tightens his grip on this role, an inner voice tells him that he cannot have that job either. In his pain, he struggles to hold on to his child. "She still needs me a little longer. I understand her better than her friends, who are as confused as she is. I will let go as soon as she can stand on her own feet. My role is just to support her a little longer. I have learned so much with the other kids that I am a better father than I have ever been. What manager would fire a player just as he is batting .500?''

It is difficult to find much satisfaction in his job as a sales manager. The people he has trained know what they are doing and seldom need him to show them how to do their tasks. His very success as a manager and teacher means that he has worked himself out of a job.

A little over a hundred years ago middle-aged people did not have this problem. There was no middle age; people were either young or old and "old" was forty. What does a man do today when he is fifty and his father career has ended and his other career has plateaued? He can increase his control over his children, or maybe can turn to an affair or to a get-rich-quick scheme.

There is another alternative which he becomes aware of only after he renounces the others. He may explore the true nature of fatherhood since that is the role he prizes most. If he is a Christian, he can ask himself what he means by God as "Father." As he explores, he will discover that God is the Father of us all, and in his case, the Father of fathers.

What kind of a Father is God anyway? Jesus said that if a son asks for a loaf of bread, what father would give him a stone, or if he asks for a fish, what father would give him a serpent? When God gives us bread, he may make it a hard rye bread which we mistake for a stone, or he may give us an eel which we mistake for a snake. The Father does not always make it easy for the child; sometimes he withdraws so the child will learn self-reliance. Sometimes he lets go and the child stumbles, but in doing so, learns to walk.

If a human father works with the idea of God as Father hard enough, he will come to a helpful conclusion. He will discover that he must decrease so that the Father can increase for the child. As the human father decreases his role, he will find that his greatest satisfaction comes as his children discover the Father of all.

The pain of "losing" a daughter or son gives way to the joy of father and child finding the Father. A transformation takes place in their relationship. They no longer have to relate as wise father leading a less experienced child. Both of them are children still being taught by a common Father. They know true equality as sons and daughters of the Father of all.

The father can have a new relationship with his children since he no longer has to take responsibility for their lives, and they no longer have to worry about pleasing him. They can meet as friends without putting demands or expectations upon each other. Paradoxically, their relationship can now become even closer because they have asked God to fill the space between them.

The father can slowly discover new possibilities in his marriage and in his job. As he and his wife find that they no longer have to take responsibility for their children, they will have more time and energy for their own relationship. As they both let go of their children, they may discover that some of the puzzling problems of parenting no longer divide them. Once in awhile each of them can play mother or father to the other, since husbands and wives sometimes need a little mothering or fathering by each other, not by their own parents.

Midlife is a time when we can turn from the expectations of others to the "still small voice of God" inside of us. We can discover the joy of occasionally doing things to please God alone. The temper checked, the new-found patience, the kind deed no one knows about except God, these all can be occasions for quiet bursts of joy. A deep satisfying glow comes as we experience such hidden satisfactions.

Finally the sales manager can see his old job in a new light. He can rejoice that he has more freedom and less stress than he would with the promotions he has been desiring. As a Christian, he can discover that helping people to receive God's joy is indeed satisfying. He certainly does not have to buttonhole his colleagues, or hard-sell his sales people. Once he is open to helping people realize that their pain can lead to joy, he will have more opportunities than he ever dreamed possible.

Then the plateau upon which his life has settled becomes a launching pad.

Chapter 10

HUMOR HEALS

There is little that is humorous about suffering, yet humor is one of the best weapons to deal with it. We sometimes visit a person in the hospital who can joke about the hospital care or about his or her own illness. We instinctively feel that suffering does not have the last word with that person. When I wrote the piece about how well my brother Wayne was facing his terminal illness he said, "It sounds like a eulogy. Don't rush me."

True, such a remark has a bit of "gallows humor" about it, but there was also a unique vantage point from which my brother viewed his illness. Sometimes he laughed to keep from crying, but Wayne's laughter revealed his faith. He could joke about my not rushing him because he believed that he was going somewhere.

A sense of humor is a sense of proportion. It says about everything, "this too shall pass away." It also says that "nothing can separate us from the love of

God," not doctors and hospitals, not even all the helpful things people try to do for us. Especially the helpful things they try to do.

A sense of humor is also a sense of our humanity—and vulnerability. It is not putting on airs or thinking we are indispensable and that God really depends upon us. A few years ago a *New Yorker* cartoon showed a group of aged executives, and one of them was saying, "It has been moved and seconded that we have ourselves frozen and return to take over in 2074."

Having a sense of humor does not mean that we are armed with a witty remark or a brilliant retort whenever we confront pain. Rather it means that we have a sense of proportion, a sense that this too will pass away. Such a sense also enables us not to pursue happiness too frantically, because that too shall pass away. Humor enables us not to be overcome by suffering.

We all suffer, but only if we are overcome by it is suffering ultimate. If we know that suffering cannot finally overcome us, we can sometimes even smile, not just keep from crying, because we have experienced a strange joy in the midst of our pain.

Humor may help us wash down a bitter pill about ourselves. A cartoon depicted a sagging, obese man seated on an examining table and the doctor saying to him, "Good grief! What have you done to the body the good Lord gave you?"

Our humor can rescue us from the disastrous results of trying to remake the world into our own image. Another cartoon showed a man walking by a stern, bearded character who had a sign that asked: "What have you done to make the world a better place today?" The man reflects for a moment, then smashes the sign over the bearded character's head and walks away with a satisfied smirk on his face.

Humor can often illuminate the underlying dread or sense of meaninglessness that lies just below the surface for many of us. If we refuse to look at our pain because it is too uncomfortable, maybe we can see it when we laugh. Jules Feiffer drew a series of sketches of a bored couple sitting opposite each other. Neither of them stirs until the man finally asks his wife, "Do you believe in life after death?" She replies, "What do you call *this?*"

Humor heals. When we are egotistical enough to assume that our sin is so great that even God cannot forgive us, the humorist punctures our pretensions. Another cartoon pictured a group of people writhing in hell with the devil stoking the flames. One tormented sinner is saying to another, "There's one thing to be said for being down here. It sure relieves those feelings of guilt."

We resist preaching because it doesn't apply to us or because it *does* apply to us. It is too painful for us affluent Americans to accept the fact that we exploit much of the rest of the world. Anyone with a sign to this effect would soon have it smashed over his head. A cartoon depicted two working men talking. One of them is saying, "By the time the meek do inherit the earth, you can bet the proud will have moved everything worthwhile to another planet."

It is equally difficult to accept sobering reality. A light touch can go further than a heavy fist. Two people are looking at a large globe of the world in a map store, and one is saying, "*There's* something they ought to declare a famous old landmark to be preserved and cherished."

The clown has often been a tragic character in drama and history. Funny people usually have an aching side to them for which their laughter is a compensation. Perhaps only those who really suffer can really laugh. Otherwise laughter becomes a matter of telling jokes, frequently obscene ones. When our humor is unconnected to our pain, it usually becomes either trivial or obscene.

The more we are willing to let our pain speak, the more humor can help us. Some people even keep their sense of humor in the midst of confusion and illness. Another cartoon pictured a doctor announcing to a patient at death's door, that "orthodox medicine has not found an answer to your complaint. However, luckily for you, I happen to be a quack."

With humor we can face the things which hurt us. Humor presupposes a vantage point from which we view ourselves and our mess. We even approach seeing ourselves as God sees us—with pathos, acceptance, mercy, and humor. When this happens we are able to transcend our fragile egos and thin skins, and that strange joy creeps in. Then we discover that laughter is indeed next to godliness, and we are not afraid to laugh and cry at the same time.

If we cannot laugh at our suffering, we can still recognize that it, too, will pass away. The most unbearable pain would be one that lasted forever, with no relief or humor. But if we believe that godliness and humor are closely related, how can there be everlasting hell or suffering without any humorous relief? This would run counter to our experience of God as a humorous Being. God is not the type to make people suffer simply for the hell of it.

The Bible speaks of God's laughing, but that is hardly sufficient evidence that he is a humorous Being. Even humorless people laugh occasionally. The humor of God lies in the way he regards us. We were created to care for the earth and to glorify him; we have done both things with a notable lack of accomplishment. That God should allow such unruly tenants to remain surely reveals his sense of humor. The irony of our seeking the gift and seldom the Giver must make God alternatively laugh and cry. God must also smile and weep as he sees us strutting about the earth seeking to dominate each other when we cannot even govern our own lives. Only a Being with a divine sense of humor would have created creatures who confuse themselves with their Creator.

In our deepest pain we need perspective. We need to know not only that this too shall pass, but that God does not like pain any more than we do. It may help to say that God allows suffering for reasons best known to him. It may help even more to remember that he suffers with us. If suffering creeps into things and he is unable to keep it out, then both God and we can laugh and cry at the irony. When we sing "For the Lord God omnipotent reigneth," perhaps God puts his hands to his face and says, "No, no, that's not quite it. I really cannot make it rain every time you want me to. I wish that I could cure your brother's cancer. I wish it as much as you do. But the problem is that, although I created all things, I do not choose to control all things. Not yet."

If this is the case, it does little good to pound at the heavenly gate or to turn our backs on God. He needs our understanding, not our rejection. If God and we both share some of the same problems, then we have the deepest possible bond between us: We can smile at each other.

Chapter 11

LITTLE DEATHS

If we human beings are distinguished from the rest of the animal kingdom by our ability to anticipate or reflect upon our own death, such a capacity is both a bane and blessing. It is painful to become aware of death, but if we are willing to endure such pain, it can also be a blessing. It is too bad that death is the last thing we do, because death can teach us so much about living. Still it takes courage to contemplate one's own death or the death of a dear one.

Death is not a single event at the end of life. It takes place gradually as we practice dying little deaths each day. It is sheer agony to die to certain dreams, not because they are bad, but because there is not time for everything. It is painful for some of us to give up the hope of becoming famous or well loved. It takes some hard swallowing to admit that we will die with only a few people realizing how kind and creative and loving we are. But to give up the hope of wide acclaim may mean that we are able to channel greater love to a few people.

The acceptance and contemplation of death need not be morbid; indeed it can open doors to a fuller joy than we ever believed possible. But, like most worthwhile things, the price is not cheap. It involves dying many times before we physically die. Jesus reminded us that "whoever would save his life will lose it, and whoever loses his life for my sake will find it."

It is painful to let go of intriguing possibilities. It is hard to convince ourselves that God does not have important work for us to do. Paradoxically, it may be just this admission which makes it possible for God to do something significant with us. Significant as he measures significance, that is.

We can pursue success until we fail and overlook the immediate, but perhaps less spectacular, things that God has in mind for us. In the pursuit of a career, husbands and wives may miss the joys of parenting. They may believe that exciting and significant things happen only outside of the family and lose the joy their children could provide. At times I wish for the prestige of a large parish. But my teen-age son's remark at the Top of the Mark on Easter, that he respected me, was more important than a thousand people saying "I enjoyed your sermon." For one thing, I am not always certain what they might mean, while I know what my son meant.

We cannot hear God's "still small voice" unless we are willing to shut out other voices clamoring for our attention. And the loudest of these voices often is our inner voice questioning whether or not we have "made it," whatever that means. We may not know the answer, but that doesn't silence the voice. The only thing that will is to die to our lust for what we call success and let God judge whether we have succeeded or not.

Dying little deaths is both difficult and endless. There is always the temptation to let up, to say to ourselves, "Now that I have died a few deaths, should I not be able to *live?*" or "If a little dying is the way to greater joy and a fuller life, then I guess it isn't so bad after all!" The problem is that we are not really dying, we are still trying to wheel and deal with God. An essential understanding of God is that he is Someone with whom we cannot wheel and deal. True dying has to be a daily, painful renunciation of our claims upon God, of our efforts to manipulate him, to get him on our side or to make faith pay off. True dying means that we are finally willing to "let God be God," as Martin Luther said.

The positive side of death is that there can be no resurrection or rebirth without it. We cannot experience new growth unless we are first willing to die. Otherwise we are like a farmer trying to plant a new crop without harvesting the old one. If I am to become alive to people's needs, then I must die to using them for my own purposes. I may not be able to turn on a switch and start loving unselfishly, but I can put an end to the little ways I use people. It is difficult to love someone if my chief thought is what they can do for me.

It is painful to die little deaths because we are never

through dying. Each day we begin anew with the struggle to die to our temper or to our selfish calculations. Each evening we realize that we still have a long way to go. But if God can be patient with us through these fits and starts, then we should be able to bear with ourselves. Fortunately, God gives us only one day at a time and, even more fortunately, he is willing to forgive us each evening.

We do not wish to die little deaths each day so we look for a quicker solution. It is painful and frustrating to grow at what seems to be an agonizingly slow pace. We are not patient people, and we expect solutions like we expect instant coffee. This is most likely to be true for some young people, or others who have not yet experienced great suffering. But most of us sense that something needs to die, something has to give, in order for new life to be born.

Chaplain Walter Johnson of Peninsula Hospital in Burlingame, California, says that he agrees with suicidal people when they say that something needs to die. But he tells them that they need not kill themselves in order to die to certain things in their lives. There can be no new life without dying, but some people confuse dying to aspects of themselves with dying to their physical selves. A person whose marriage has failed needs to find assurance that this does not make him or her a failure as a person. Divorce often causes people to reexamine their lives and see, as they never could before, what needs to die in order that other things may be born. Without the pain of marital problems, they might never have seen these things.

Suicide closes the door on possible growth. The person is saying either that pain has nothing to say, or that it is too painful to listen to it any longer. But how can we know that our pain has nothing more to teach us, or when our suffering will give way to a strange joy? Jesus was ready to have his pain end when he prayed in Gethsemane, but God had more to say to him and to the world. We would never have heard Jesus' words of love and forgiveness for his enemies if it were not for the cross. Neither would we have known his feelings of abandonment and then heard his words of final resignation to God. Most of all, we would not know the strange joy of Easter if it were not for the suffering of Good Friday.

Suicide may result from a deafness to what the pain is saying. If pain only causes pain, then our suffering is pointless. And since pain has such a bad name in our society, most of us have trouble believing that any good can come of it. It is the faith that our suffering is not in vain which gives us the courage to keep listening.

Often suicide is a premature, impulsive act like when someone throws a supposedly broken portable radio into the trash, only to have it start playing when it lands. With some suicides, it is not the pain, but the frustration, which is unbearable. If these people could have held on longer, they might have broken through the anguish. Instead of literally killing them, the pain could have matured them. There is evidence of this from the number of people saved from suicide who go on to live creative lives. Later many say how glad they were to be rescued.

Some people have had little pain or have always blocked it out mentally and have not listened to it. Such people are likely to feel overwhelmed if great pain suddenly strikes them. Those who let their pain speak and understand what it says are in a position to deal with greater pain when it comes to them. Likewise, people who have experienced dying "little deaths" or defeats know that their physical selves need not die for a part of them to die. One of the reasons that the suicide rate is high among young people is that often they have not had much experience in dying little deaths, in learning that "this too shall pass away."

Suffering visibly breaks some people while it strengthens others. The difference is not so much in the degree of pain, but in our response to it. If we believe that pain is to be avoided at all costs, then suicide might be a logical response. If we believe that pain usually has something to teach us, that it is not a sign of God's rejection or disapproval, then we are enabled to endure much suffering, not because we are martyrs or masochists, but because we want to gain every bit of wisdom we can. We desire to squeeze every drop of good from our pain. We even dare to expect that a strange joy will follow our agony.

The notion of accepting pain for what it can teach has no part in a culture of comfort and immediate satisfaction. Delayed satisfaction, to say nothing of endured suffering, does not fit our way of life. God is expected to guarantee full satisfaction with every life he creates. If this does not happen, then why not return the life to him? Suicide is a way of expressing dissatisfaction with the way life has turned out, a protest against life's obvious injustices and inequities. But whoever said life was supposed to be just? The world perhaps, but not our Christian faith. The suffering and death of Jesus were hardly just; the most innocent life suffered capital punishment.

Looking at Jesus' rejection, even by his closest friends, and his completely unjust sentence, reveals how he dealt with pain. He did not remove himself from it, rather he turned his face to it. Then he squeezed the last drop of wisdom from his pain. Jesus could not have been on a suicidal mission, as some writers have suggested, because that would have meant stilling his pain. Jesus came to reveal life in its fullest, and part of that fullness meant waiting out the pain. He prayed that the cup might be taken from him, but when he saw that his suffering had more to say to the world and even to himself, he endured.

> Therefore, since we are surrounded by so great a cloud of witnesses, let us also lay aside every weight, and sin which clings so closely, and let us run with perseverance the race that is set before us, looking to Jesus the pioneer and perfecter of our faith, who for the joy that was set before him endured the cross, despising the shame, and is seated at the right hand of the throne of God.

It was a strange joy which could motivate someone

to go through the agony of a criminal's death. But Jesus was already practiced in dying little deaths as he surrendered daily to the Father's will. When the ultimate test came, he was ready. Above all, he had already experienced the joy of obedience in small things, so he anticipated the greater joy of being faithful in a large thing.

Chapter 12

SUFFICIENT GRACE

And to keep me from being too elated by the abundance of revelations, a thorn was given me in the flesh, a messenger of Satan, to harass me, to keep me from being too elated. Three times I besought the Lord about this, that it should leave me; but he said to me, "My grace is sufficient for you, for my power is made perfect in weakness." I will all the more gladly boast of my weaknesses, that the power of Christ may rest upon me. For the sake of Christ, then, I am content with weaknesses, insults, hardships, persecutions, and calamities; for when I am weak, then I am strong.

The notion that God uses pain and suffering as a means of revealing his grace and power is a difficult one for most of us. We can believe that God's grace is functioning when we pray to get well and do. But to say that God ignores our requests in order to demonstrate his grace and power seems a rationalization. Yet this is what Paul meant when he said, "for when I am weak, then I am strong."

God's grace, or unearned favor, enabled Paul to hear the pain out, to discern what it was saying to him.

God's grace was "sufficient," not just to bear the suffering, but to learn from it. And he discovered a strange strength in his weakness. Without the "thorn in the flesh" he would not have discovered his need for a grace which is sufficient. Grace made it possible for Paul to endure the suffering and to discover power in weakness.

Without his thorn, Paul would not have known the strength he speaks about. Paul was not a masochist; three times he begged the Lord to take his "thorn" from him. Finally, he concluded that the pain was there for a purpose, "to keep me from becoming too elated." Perhaps most of us are not troubled by too much elation, but it is easy for us to feel self-sufficient as long as everything is going well for us.

If Paul had received stoic strength to bear his pain, his would have been a graceless suffering. He could have only concluded that his pain was meaningless, the result of a bad throw of the dice. Instead he discovered that pain is a means by which God reveals his power.

The difference between graceless and grace-filled suffering is the final conviction that God can bring good out of evil. God may not have given Paul the thorn in his flesh, but he wished to use it for Paul's good. If Paul had insisted that only the removal of the thorn could be good, he would not have discovered the power hidden in weakness.

By grace, Paul knew how to be abased as well as how to be elated; he could accept a different answer than the one he desired. Still it was not easy for him to resign himself to his pain, so he prayed for its removal. But finally, by grace, he was willing to listen to the Voice speaking through his suffering.

Grace and power come to us as we are willing to admit that we do not know what is best for us. Christian maturity is admitting that the answer we pray for is not necessarily the answer we need. A new kind of power comes to us as we are willing to relinquish the old power we have claimed over our lives. It is Jesus' paradox of gaining our lives by losing them.

By grace, we discover that success or failure, sickness or health, pain or pleasure, even good or evil do not determine God's love for us. "Whether we live or whether we die, we are the Lord's," Paul concluded. When we come to this realization, nothing can separate us from the love of God. Whatever happens becomes a means of grace, an occasion through which God can speak to us.

When we suffer the pangs of remorse and guilt, God uses this pain to reveal his forgiveness. He shows us that no matter what has happened in the past, it need not contaminate or determine the present. We are reborn each day. Because God accepts and loves us as we are, we can become what he intended us to be.

Grace and power come to us not despite the suffering, but often because of it. As he felt the terrifying thrust of nails tearing flesh, Jesus cried out to God, asking why he had forsaken him. But Jesus addressed the question to God, not to the thin air. And in suffering on the cross, Jesus received sufficient grace to commit himself finally into the hands of God. The physical suffering was little compared to the agony he would have felt if he found no hands to receive him.

God's grace is sufficient when we know that God can use whatever happens to us as the raw material for wisdom and joy. We no longer have to suffer the greatest agony of all, of thinking that our pain is in vain. As we go through pain to the other side, we experience a strange joy.

Grace means that our ability to grow in wisdom is not dependent upon what we do. We grow "in our sleep, . . . in our own despair, against our will. . . ." If it had been left up to Paul, the thorn would have been removed, and he would have been finished with the whole business. Instead, God left the thorn and gave Paul sufficient grace to receive "power made perfect in weakness."

That grace can be awe-full is something that we do not readily perceive. For most of us grace is something pleasant, like pardon and a new chance, like renewed courage and strength. It is these, to be sure, but grace often comes with "pain which cannot forget." For many of us grace comes painfully before we experience its pardon and renewal. It is "amazing grace" because it comes to us in unexpected ways, but seldom without pain. If grace came too cheaply or painlessly, we might well suspect it. We cannot earn grace by our suffering, rather grace comes to us, against our will, bringing wisdom and a strange joy as its gifts. But like the birth of a baby, these gifts are preceded by travail.

If God were the president of the Bank of America, he would break it in a day. He would constantly make loans to people whose only qualification was that they had blown their last loan at Las·Vegas.

God continually pours out his grace like a mad banker. He gives it to those of us who show absolutely no talent for using it wisely. After we have squandered his grace, we feel stabs of pain as we become aware of wasted years and talents. Yet even this awareness is a sign of grace.

For the believer, the stabs of pain also reveal God's love. "For the Lord disciplines him whom he loves, and chastises every son whom he receives." God's grace is given freely without any striving or merit on our part, but grace can be hard, and God's love is stern. As Dietrich Bonhoeffer noted, grace is not "cheap."

Still grace is poured out without ceasing. The constancy of it causes us pain as we contrast our unfaithfulness with God's faithfulness.

There are also pains of warning as we experience that God is not mocked. We think of grace as God's endless mercy, but "endless mercy" is not really merciful. Not if it lets us stagnate and suffocate in our sin. *Because* the Lord is merciful, he will not indulge our pride or indolence forever.

> The Lord is merciful and gracious,
>   slow to anger and abounding in
>   steadfast love.
>
> He will not always chide,
>   nor will he keep his anger
>   for ever.

It is painful to realize that God's mercy means that he will not "keep his anger forever." Still our suffering produces joy as we sense that God cares enough about us to warn us. Painfully.

We experience anguish as we disobey or, perhaps more commonly today, ignore God. But this is nothing compared to the anguish of looking back over a life of "if only's" and "it might have been's." Just as a parent shows mercy by punishing a child who plays with fire, so the Lord "chastises every son whom he receives."

It is not difficult to praise God for his mercies which "are new every morning," but it is difficult to praise him for our anguish. Few of us seek pain, and we do not usually think of suffering as part of God's mercy.

But by grace, we are slowly made aware that it is through pain that we are made whole.

Chapter 13

THE ULTIMATE THERAPY

Like most primitive tribes, the boys in the neighborhood where I grew up had a rite of initiation. They would challenge each new boy to a fight. This could be a one-on-one affair or, if the newcomer looked formidable, they might gang up on him. There was no way to escape or run away from this ritual. Since our parents forbade us to fight, my brothers and I were regularly waylaid as we walked home. It was like being on combat patrol; we could expect to be ambushed at any moment.

After the pain and humiliation of countless such encounters, it would seem reasonable that we would become sensitive to the plight of another weak kid. Wrong. We found a gawky, shy boy who lived several blocks away and made him our victim. When the kids on our block beat us up, we would hunt Arvid Setren down and take out our pain and frustration on him. His awkward, fumbling efforts to get away were just like the ones we made when the gang terrorized us. I can still remember his frightened, pleading eyes as he asked only to be left alone. Later Arvid was one of the first boys in our Washburn High School class of 1942 to be killed in World War II.

Why is it that we could inflict on someone else the same pain we ourselves suffered? Why did our suffering make us cruel instead of compassionate? Is there not any way to stop this chain reaction of pain causing pain? "The ultimate therapy," according to Parker J. Palmer, a Quaker teacher, "is to identify our pain with the pain of others." It is ultimate therapy because it helps heal both them and us.

Jesus, who is himself the Good News, absorbed pain: "When he was reviled, he did not revile in return; when he suffered, he did not threaten; but he trusted to him who judges justly." Something happened when pain fell drop by drop upon Jesus' heart. He received pain until he gained wisdom. Then he could feel the pain of others. He could even pray for those who were tormenting him because he identified his pain with theirs.

Still, how do we stop the cycle of pain causing pain? To be sure, we each gain wisdom in different ways. One little boy who moved into our neighborhood after we did demonstrated deep wisdom. Perhaps he had suffered at the hands of other bullies and knew the futility of continuing the pain. When a gang member challenged him, he said, "You're bigger than me, so if you want to beat me up, you can." The bully unclenched his fists and walked away. This wise little boy did not join the rest of us in tormenting Arvid. He had identified his pain with the pain of another.

When some of us suffer, our pain never reaches our hearts. In others suffering works in their hearts until wisdom comes. The little boy who said, "If you want to beat me up, you can," was wise and peaceful. The rest of us were nonviolent only with those who could whip us, but violent with weaker people like Arvid. This little boy's pain had taught him wisdom, while our pain had not yet reached into our hearts.

When Jesus was reviled and did not revile in return, and when he suffered and did not threaten, it was because pain had produced a wisdom about God and life within him. He "trusted to him who judges justly." He knew that God was not causing his suffering, and he knew that his Father would judge those who caused it. Jesus did not have to find an Arvid to strike out against in blind pain. Instead he prayed for those who tortured him.

If we regard pain as an enemy, we will have a low tolerance for suffering and frustration. We will be unwilling to let the pain sink in deep enough to give its message to us. When we begin with the assumption that suffering itself is evil, it is difficult to learn very much from it. However, if suffering is a "means of grace," then we may receive its wisdom, even against our will.

Children frequently suffer at the hands of their parents. When parents haven't listened to their own pain, their children often suffer their parents' unheeded pain. Instead of making them wise, the parents' neglected pain makes them cruel. The cycle of pain passed down from generation to generation will continue until, by the grace of God, someone cries out, "I know that I have been treated unjustly by my father, and that he was also treated harshly by his father, but that does not excuse my father's behavior or mine. I am angry at him, but I am also angry over the way pain is blindly passed down from one generation to another. I am angry and hurt enough to do something about this. The pain stops here. I will not do this to my children. Their pain is now my pain."

Wisdom comes despite us because we naturally resist pain. When we endure pain by grace, healing and joy follow. When the Samaritan treated the traveler he poured wine on his wounds—it hurt, but it also cleansed. Had the traveler insisted that he did not want to be hurt anymore, he could not have been healed.

The child who is being physically or spiritually abused by a parent does not have the experience to know that his or her suffering is not a total loss. If the abuse is great enough (How would we measure this?) the child should be separated from the parent. Unfortunately, this is often impossible, even in extreme cases. Besides, most of us can think of instances when we suffered unfairly at the hands of our parents. It was a terrifying feeling, since our parents were so powerful and we were so vulnerable. All we could do was hope and pray that they would ease up on us. We were afraid to pray that they leave us alone, for that meant rejection. And rejection seemed like the most painful thing of all.

As mistreated children we could think of little else than our parents' cruel temper. We longed for the day when we would be liberated from it, but that day never seemed to come. Then finally we were able to leave our parents and establish our own homes. Will we fall into the same parental patterns we learned as children? After all, parents are expected to exercise control over their children and control often means force. And what if the only force we knew involved abuse, even brutality? Much of what we know we have learned by example, so it is difficult to discipline our children in ways different than we ourselves experienced.

In the movie, *I Never Sang for My Father*, suffering was not discovered as a means of grace. The father was still bitter about his own father who drank and who had left his wife and young children. When he grew up and had his own family, instead of rejoicing that his children did not have to suffer as he did, he allowed bitterness to infect his relationship with his children. Obviously, the pain had not reached his heart, and he had not seen himself in the pained expressions of his own children.

It is necessary to endure a while without demanding an instant payoff from our suffering. Sometimes we are too immature or feel too downcast to think about any long-range, positive results. Perhaps at times we suffer without the hope of any good's coming from it, but our endurance is seldom in vain. It may be that our reward will come years later, as when a son who was oppressed by his father determines to develop a warm relationship with his own sons. This relationship will not come automatically or simply by luck. It will come because drop by drop the pain is reaching into the father's heart as he remembers what it felt like to be abused as a child. When the pain floods his own heart, the father will refuse to abuse his own children in the same fashion. The fact that often brutal parents were once brutalized children means that these parents have not broken through to the other side of their pain. Perhaps they have been unwilling to listen long enough to their own pain. We cannot force grace; it comes despite us, but we can accept the fact that wisdom comes only through suffering.

The hope is that our pain will soak in. All of our instincts rebel against feeling again the hurt we felt as children. We struggle to forget or repress our pain, but pain is never really forgotten; it is covered over with protective layers. And "in our sleep, against our will" our pain soaks into our hearts. There is no inexorable law saying that because we were hurt, we must hurt in return. The gospel means that suffering can produce sensitivity, patience, and kindness, not necessarily more suffering. We break through to the other side of the pain and experience the awful grace of God when we see ourselves in others and recognize the pain on their faces as our own.

The drops keep falling until by the grace of God, some wisdom comes. As a child I often dragged my feet getting off to school in the morning. When it was apparent that I would get there late, my father would rush me to school. On the way he would furiously berate me. Once at school, it was difficult to concentrate on my lessons as by brain swirled with his rebukes. Although wisdom came too late for me to change my tardy ways, I learned a lesson I could apply to my children. I vowed that I would never do this to my kids. I would either let them walk and suffer the consequences of being late, or, if I drove them, I would never drop them off hurt by my words. Now, as a father of four grown children, I have been angry with them at times, but never before school, and the pennies of suffering as a child have been repaid me in gold coins of joy as a parent.

Sometimes when I overreacted with my children, I caught the pain in their eyes. Their looks aroused the despair I felt as a child crouched in the corner of the car, listening to my father rave. As I felt my old pain again, wisdom came through God's awful grace, and I was made aware of my children's pain. As I felt my pain, I experienced the joy of their loving me even when I was unlovable.

Even though we often perpetuate the sins of our parents, this does not always have to be so. Not if our pain has soaked into our hearts and done its work. The tragedy is that it often takes a lifetime for us to learn from our agony. Life is so short, and we are so stubborn. But God continues to work against our will.

The healing of our pain is not complete until we

have identified it with the pain of others. Often the reaction to pain is to make someone else suffer for our hurt. If it cannot be the person who inflicted pain upon us, we hunt for a weaker person to punish. This is our first reaction before pain reaches the heart. But the pain drops continue, in our sleep, against our will until one day we wake up and see Arvid's pleading eyes, and we discover that we are looking into a mirror.

It is against our will to identify our pain with the pain of others. Many of us are Christians because we know that we cannot do this by ourselves. First, our bruised and battered psyches need to be healed from within by the Ultimate Healer. Otherwise our efforts to make the pain stop with us, to keep from passing it on to others, have all the permanency of New Year's resolutions.

It isn't enough that the pain drops keep falling upon the heart, unless along with these drops of pain there is also God's healing grace. We cannot earn this grace; we can only yearn for it. But the very yearning for it is a sign that the healing has already begun in us.

As we recognize our powerlessness over our stubborn natures and our inability to keep from passing pain on to others, something begins to break loose inside of us. The old moorings give way, our confidence is broken, and we feel our pain in a new way. We know that more will power or more self-discipline will not make us more loving. Then slowly we experience the painful grace of God doing for us what we cannot do for ourselves. After knowing the pain of being lost, we discover the joy of being found.

Perhaps your experience is something like mine. As my pain gets to be too much, I beg God to heal me. Then, like the nine healed lepers, I quickly forget the Healer and go about my business—until pain starts gnawing away again. Finally, I learn that my pain is not the opposite of grace, but part of it. *I discover that not all pain is graceful, but that all grace is painful.*

Sometimes I am open to healing as I reflect alone before God upon my betrayals, my callousness toward the pain of others, the Arvids I have run over. Other times I become painfully aware of my need for help as someone diagnoses my problem for me. The Holy Spirit takes a peculiar delight in speaking to me through my wife. My quickness to defend myself is usually a measure of the truth she has spoken. (This insight I will promptly forget the next time she touches a sensitive nerve.)

The promise beyond the pain is fulfilled when we realize how God's sustaining love takes care of each one of us. The strange joy is not how well we hang on to God, but how well he hangs on to us.

REFERENCES

Psalm 126:5 (KJV).......................... Dedication page
John 17:3... p: 18, ¶ 1
John 4:34.. p: 19, ¶ 1
Matthew 26:39 (GNB)............................. p: 19, ¶ 1
Matthew 16:25... p: 20
2 Corinthians 5:19.................................. p: 42, ¶ 2
Romans 8:16-17...................................... p: 46, ¶ 3
Matthew 27:46.. p: 51, ¶ 3
Romans 7:19.. p: 53, ¶ 2
Matthew 12:45.. p: 54
2 Corinthians 12:7-9.............................. p: 54, ¶ 1
Luke 23:46.. p: 56
Hebrews 12:1-2....................................... p: 67, ¶ 2
Psalm 51:4.. p: 74, ¶ 1
Romans 7:24-25 (NEB)............................ p: 74, ¶ 3
Isaiah 6:7... p: 75
Hebrews 12:1-2....................................... p: 93, ¶ 1
2 Corinthians 12:7-10............................ p: 95
Hebrews 12:6.. p: 99, ¶ 3
Psalm 103:8-9... p: 99, ¶ 5
1 Peter 2:23.. p: 102, ¶ 2